TEN
GARMENTS
every man
should own

PEDRO MENDES

TEN GARMENTS
every man should own

A Practical Guide to
Building a Permanent Wardrobe

DUNDURN
TORONTO

Publisher and acquiring editor: Scott Fraser | Editor: Kate Unrau
Cover and interior designer: Laura Boyle
Cover image: istockphoto.com/saemilee
Interior illustrations: Firdaus Ahmed
Printer: Friesens

Library and Archives Canada Cataloguing in Publication

Title: Ten garments every man should own : a practical guide to building a permanent wardrobe / Pedro Mendes.
Names: Mendes, Pedro, 1971- author.
Description: Includes bibliographical references.
Identifiers: Canadiana (print) 20200323482 | Canadiana (ebook) 20200323512 | ISBN 9781459747463 (hardcover) | ISBN 9781459747470 (PDF) | ISBN 9781459747487 (EPUB)
Subjects: LCSH: Men's clothing. | LCSH: Fashion.
Classification: LCC TT617 .M46 2021 | DDC 646.4/02—dc23

We acknowledge the support of the Canada Council for the Arts and the Ontario Arts Council for our publishing program. We also acknowledge the financial support of the Government of Ontario, through the Ontario Book Publishing Tax Credit and Ontario Creates, and the Government of Canada.

Care has been taken to trace the ownership of copyright material used in this book. The author and the publisher welcome any information enabling them to rectify any references or credits in subsequent editions.

The publisher is not responsible for websites or their content unless they are owned by the publisher.

Printed and bound in Canada.

VISIT US AT

 dundurn.com | @dundurnpress | dundurnpress | dundurnpress

Dundurn Press
1382 Queen Street East
Toronto, Ontario, Canada
M4L 1C9

For Jonah

CONTENTS

Why This Matters

The world is drowning in clothes. Some estimates suggest that one hundred billion garments are produced every year. That's over a dozen for each person on earth, which is four times as many as just twenty years ago. This is a problem because of the massive amounts of energy and resources, like water, being used to manufacture and ship all this clothing. But the problem doesn't end there. Much of this glut of clothing does not even last a year and ends up in landfills. Approximately thirteen million tons worth, which is about twice the weight of the Great Pyramid of Giza. In other words, clothing is no longer owned, it is consumed. And that has to change.

That may sound like a strange intro to a book about buying clothes, especially if you are expecting pages full of shopping lists and "must haves" for the different seasons. But I've learned that clothing matters much more than that. When I first decided to change my wardrobe from whatever was on sale at the mall to classic menswear, I was working as a CBC Radio producer. I had the luxury of not only learning about clothes, but also making documentaries along the way. This gave me an excuse, in search of story material, to spend long hours in tailor shops and crafts-people's studios. In fact, I've travelled all around North America and Europe meeting and learning from artisans: tailors in New York, shirt makers in Bologna, shoemakers in Paris. If I had just been commissioning garments, I could never have afforded that education. Plus, most people don't ask their tailor for their life story while getting an inseam measured. Journalism allowed me to go deeper than the fabric or the design, to uncover essential truths about the clothes we wear.

That is why I believe there is, if not a solution, a path toward a better relationship with our clothing. A path that is better for the environment and garment workers. And a path that will give us more enjoyment and a deeper, more satisfying connection with our wardrobes. The solution is to buy less but buy better. You've probably heard that before, and it might even make you roll your eyes. What does "buy less but buy better" even mean? And how do you do it? The point of this book is to guide you toward actually achieving that ideal. The result is not only a sustainable wardrobe but also a discovery of the true joy of dressing.

Buy Less

It's easy enough to buy less. Well, it should be. Just stop buying so many clothes. If we did — if the average person in a developed country wore garments for two years instead of the now-common one year, we would cumulatively have a massive positive impact on the environment. Buying less is also a way to mitigate certain negative factors in the production of clothing. For instance, even though cotton is a natural fibre, its production requires an enormous amount of fresh water that could be otherwise used for drinking and agriculture in developing countries. Even worse is leather, which is probably the most environmentally destructive clothing material in the world due to the toxic chemicals used in the tanning process. And then there's the issue of animal welfare: some natural materials are a by-product of the food industry (leather) or harvested from living animals (wool). And so the onus is on us to keep that usage ethical (which can be subjective, I know) and as minimally impactful as possible.

However, if we purchased fewer jackets, fewer cotton shirts, and fewer leather shoes, and if we make them last longer, the overall impact would be lessened. We can offset the environmental impact of production by getting a longer life out of each garment. Fewer would be made, so on the whole, the global effect would be smaller.

But even though buying less sounds simple, it isn't. Not when there are so many options for cheap, fashionable clothes. Here's one strategy that might help: promise to never throw away a piece of wearable clothes again. Don't even let it be an option. Before you buy something, consider the life of the garment: What else can you do with it when you no longer want it? Is it just bound for a landfill because it won't last or because it is made of synthetic materials? What effect will this extra thought have on you while you're browsing at a department store or scanning through items online?

To buy less, I also use the "one in/one out" system. If I have all the essentials covered in my wardrobe and something new enters my life, something old must go. So I need to be ready to part with that item — and to find it a good new home. For example, I currently have half a dozen sport jackets, and I love them all. The one in/one out system keeps me from buying any more sport jackets because if I did, I'd have to part with one I already own. And since I'm not simply going to throw away an old one if I do decide to bring in something new, the onus and responsibility is on me to figure out what to do with the old jacket. Donating to charity or finding a used store is always an option, but with the glut of used clothing in the world, these are not foolproof plans.

Another strategy for buying less is to spend more money than you are comfortable spending. You can find plenty of shirts for twenty dollars, but if you commit to never spending less than $150 on a shirt, then chances are you will do everything you can to ensure that shirt is of good quality, that it suits your wardrobe, that it is something you actually need, and that you take good care of it to make it last as long as possible.

Where Does Cost Come From?

There are three main factors I think about when it comes to the cost of any item: raw materials, design, and construction. Investment by the maker in all three elements should determine price, so the easiest way to lower the price is to invest less in any or all three. For example, using lower-quality materials (e.g., lower-grade leather, wool, cotton). Or investing little in design (i.e., stock patterns for garments that end up fitting poorly). Or scrimping on the machinery and/or time necessary to make the garment. This also includes, sadly, paying low wages and not investing in worker safety, skills, and development. A low cost always comes from somewhere, and it is rarely a company's profits.

Buy Better

This part of the equation is much trickier because how do you "buy better"? In my opinion, a wardrobe based on quality, made of fabrics that will last, is the key to buying better. And it isn't necessarily about spending more money; it's about spending more time. Time spent on researching makers and fabrics, learning how to identify quality, and then searching it out. This means slowing down the process of buying clothes — just one way to take the *fast* out of "fast fashion."

Here's what that actually looks like in day-to-day practice. When you are thinking about buying a garment, you must place suitability above whim. Despite how it looks, does this item actually fit in to your life and wardrobe? So, think about your lifestyle: do you spend most of your time in an office, at home, or outdoors? Think about your climate: is it moderate, extreme, rainy, or dry? And, of course, think about your personal style. This will involve some introspection and self-knowledge, but a good start is to look at the rest of your wardrobe. Does the new item actually fill a gap in your wardrobe? Does it harmonize with the rest of your clothes?

Another strategy I use to be more judicious with my shopping is to create a cloud-based wish list of the items I'd like in my wardrobe. These are items I've already given serious thought and consideration to, and because the list is in the cloud, I can access it from my phone anywhere. That way, when I'm shopping, I can focus on what I've

> Don't buy a bunch of "dry clean only" clothes if you never go to a dry cleaner. Don't buy "handwash only" if you never handwash. Then again, read the section "Caring for Your Wardrobe," and let me introduce you to the joy of handwashing and clothing maintenance.

already thought through and planned. Then, of course, once I've bought them, I need to care for those garments (see "Caring for Your Wardrobe").

Most importantly, buying better means considering the impact your purchase is having on the world around you. Is the garment made of a natural, sustainable product? Was it made in a facility or country that is responsible when it comes to environmental and working standards? These are difficult questions to answer, I know, and I'll go into more detail, garment by garment, throughout this book. You might already be thinking about these issues when it comes to the food you eat, in other words, what goes *in* your body: Where was it grown? How was it prepared? Who did that work under what conditions? But it's time to start asking those questions about what goes *on* your body.

What Is Value?

The way a piece of clothing makes you feel isn't necessarily connected to the price you paid or even to the quality. Value can be intangible and highly personal. At least it is for me. The biggest value I place on my wardrobe doesn't come from how it was made or where, but how it makes me feel. And that has a lot to do with defining, for me, what masculinity and being a grown-up mean.

I remember one night trying to put my son to sleep when he was just nine months old. He looked at me in that way only babies do, deep into my soul (although he was probably just trying to pass gas). I realized in that moment what I was: not just his father, but his primary role model for what a grown man can be. And I had no idea what that meant.

I was part of a generation that held on to adolescence for as long as possible. I was distrustful of "growing up" and maturity, while at the same time desperately aware of what I was lacking when it came to basic life skills and the confidence that comes with them. So, looking at my son that evening I committed myself to making a change. I would face my anxieties and do everything I could to live each day as a better person than I was the day before. One of my strategies was to change what was outside in the hopes of changing what was inside. I would start learning about clothing and dressing with intent, in the hopes that it would help me in other parts of my life.

But as soon as I started making this change, as soon as I started paying attention to my clothes, people began calling me out. I was accused of being superficial. Told that it wasn't manly to be concerned with appearance. Then there was the everyday, endless stream of jokes about weddings and job interviews I might be attending.

This is, I think, a reflection of a deep-seated misogyny in our culture that equates ostentation with femininity. And since it is still considered, by some, less masculine to express any femininity, a man paying attention to his appearance is considered a negative. But the more I learned about clothing, the more I dug into the past, the more I realized how strange and wrong these views are.

Until recently, even into the 1960s, concern with one's appearance was a sign of maturity. Not anything foppish, like spending hours in front of the mirror. But consider that the first building usually erected in a Wild West town was a barbershop. Men cared for and enjoyed expressing themselves through their clothes. That was masculine; that was manly. Over the last few decades, many men have lost that joy and expressiveness, despite how progressive we might be in other aspects of society.

The value I've discovered in my clothes is not just the feeling of confidence it gives me; it's the freedom I enjoy to express a side of myself that used to be closed off. It's a realization that classic menswear, despite some people thinking it is retrograde, actually gives me permission to express a new level of masculinity. My clothes are an expression of my joy, not just the other way around.

> Why is it more acceptable for men to spend untold amounts of time (and sometimes money) obsessing over cars or sports equipment than over their own clothing? This shift in values goes hand in hand with the decline in clothing quality, not formality.

Equally important has been learning that "value" does not mean low cost. In terms of price, value is the ratio between cost and quality. A high-quality item at a low cost has a high value. A low-quality item at a low cost has a low value. I place quality of materials and construction along with a good fit above the look of an item and even the price. Don't let low prices and flashy looks sway you.

Value is also related to time. As an item ages, its value is increased the longer it lasts, if it actually improves with age, or if it can be repaired. But that process of breaking in, becoming more comfortable, even developing a patina depends on you and the satisfying work of maintenance (see "Caring for Your Wardrobe").

"Classic"

I'm quite aware that what I call "classic" some people would call old-fashioned or retro. But I am not interested in living in the past. This book is not a guide for vintage wear. However, when it comes to clothes, we can learn a lot from the past that can help us face the problems of the here and now. Values like quality and care go a long way to addressing the social, economic, and environmental quagmires the world of fast fashion has thrust us into.

In the early to mid-twentieth century, men's clothing was ruled by three simple guidelines: moderation in style, quality of construction, and a comfortable, flattering fit. Yes, comfort. This was a generation that replaced stiff, starched collars with soft button-downs, tall boots with loafers, and structured frock coats with soft tweeds. And a vast number of stores and tailors could be relied upon to deliver these new types of clothing. I recently spoke to a gentleman in his nineties who has been a menswear salesman most of his life. I was desperate to know if, back in the 1950s and 60s, the average man knew much more about clothing than guys know today. What he told me was a revelation to me: They didn't. Not really. They were more familiar with terms like "cutaway" and "brogue" and knew they wanted to dress a certain way, but they had little idea how to get there. Or all the minutiae of men's tailoring to build such a wardrobe. The difference was, this guy told me, that in those days salespeople could be relied upon to give excellent guidance and advice. Their goal was to build a relationship by providing dependable, personal service, not a quick sale to get your money and get you out the door. Plus, the garments available in most stores were well made and neither too fashionable nor out of fashion. That combination is extremely hard to find in the twenty-first century.

In fact, in the last few decades, we have seen a race toward bargain-basement prices, disposable items, and the seasonal whims of fashion. The latter, which has sadly been the bailiwick of women for over a century, is increasingly the choice men face, as well. Fashion cycles change seasonally, if not monthly. Unrealistic, damaging pressures are placed on body shape and body image. And an unrelenting barrage of advertisements and Instagram posts about clothing focus purely on design and say nothing about quality.

The result is a generation of men who have little to no connection to their clothes: they don't know where to buy them, they don't know how they should fit, and they don't know how to take care of them. They spend more money replacing throw-away clothing than they would on lasting, quality pieces. They contribute to poor working conditions (often unknowingly), environmental toxins, and the topping up of landfills. And their clothes no longer express a sense of self that is unique and different from the images spat out at them from social media and magazines. Learning how to build a quality wardrobe will address all of these problems.

Even though the focus of this book is classic menswear, I'm not saying that tailored clothing is inherently more sustainable than other styles. With a lack of care and attention, you might easily amass a large wardrobe of flimsy, disposable suits and leather shoes. I do believe, though, that classic, tailored clothing has the best options for a sustainable wardrobe because of its focus on natural materials, high levels of craftsmanship, and styles that will last decades. It is literally "slow fashion": you build your wardrobe gradually over time as you learn and you add items you need judiciously, from garments that are made one at a time, with care.

I will gladly — but not proudly — admit that I don't always follow my own advice. Sometimes I end up with things in my wardrobe that are mistakes. They don't work with other garments, the fit isn't quite right, or they're just not my style. Perhaps I bought them on a whim or because I rushed or they were on sale. But we learn from our mistakes. I've learned that unless I am careful and patient and deliberate and thoughtful, I end up with clothes I neither like nor wear. I know I will continue to be impulsive and foolhardy, because that is who I am. But perhaps, thanks to these missteps, I'll be a little bit less impulsive and foolhardy. As a result, I try not to see these purchases as failures, especially because I commit myself to finding a good second home for them.

And finally, the goal of this book is not to get you to dress like me. In fact, all I want is for you to dress better than you do now, in other words, a better version of what you already wear:

better quality, better fit, more thoughtful, more sustainable. Most importantly, I want you to develop a new relationship with your clothing. I want you to invest personally in your clothing so that you have an emotional connection to what you wear. And an ongoing sense of enjoyment every time you open your closet rather than just a fleeting and temporary source of dopamine when you buy your clothes. Because getting dressed shouldn't be a chore or a worry or a challenge. It should be a joy.

Leather Shoes

*Cheap shoes look cheap even when they're new, but
good shoes look good even when they're old.*
— G. Bruce Boyer

As the foundation of any outfit, shoes can teach you a lot about how to acquire and care for your entire wardrobe. A few pairs of good-quality all-leather shoes will last for years, if not decades; harmonize with a wide range of outfits and activities; and be a vehicle for learning about wardrobe maintenance. But I'll be honest: building a shoe collection is hard work because of all the options and makers. Before I get into all that, though, let me explain the types of shoes I'm talking about.

By the 1930s, the styles I suggest in this chapter — oxfords, derbies, monks, and loafers — had all been well established. Standard pairs look almost identical to what is being sold today, except for subtle things like silhouette and decoration. And those change mostly from maker to maker, not so much over time. Perhaps because they are so useful while not extreme in design, classic leather shoes seem to escape the fluctuations of fashion unlike any other garment. That alone makes them well worth an investment.

Quality

Before we get down to the nuts and bolts of leather shoes, the overarching argument is that you need to invest in quality. This is much easier said than done. Most of us have grown accustomed — and not just with shoes — to poor quality. There has been a rush to the bottom in the mass-market footwear industry, and most customers are unaware of how flimsy and poorly made their shoes are until the shoes start to fall apart after a short time. Even then, we are so used to it, and the shoes are so cheap, that we just buy another pair. And over time we spend a fair amount of money topping up landfills and unknowingly promoting poor working conditions.

Consider, first, the materials that go into a shoe. Various types of leather are used for different purposes: the upper, the sole, the internal structure, the lining. Other materials — cork, metal, and thread — also form the structure of the shoe. Many of these are never seen by the customer, so it is easy for manufacturers to replace them with lesser-quality items, but some makers do not compromise. Quality makers source the best leathers they can, from the finest tanneries. Then they use some hand labour along with highly skilled mechanical techniques to construct the shoes. They do all this because they want to make shoes that are not only durable but also comfortable and stylish. Most of all, these shoes are imbued with their creative vision, in the silhouette and finishing.

If a maker is going to take the high road and do everything to the best of their ability, there is a cost associated. Cost usually,

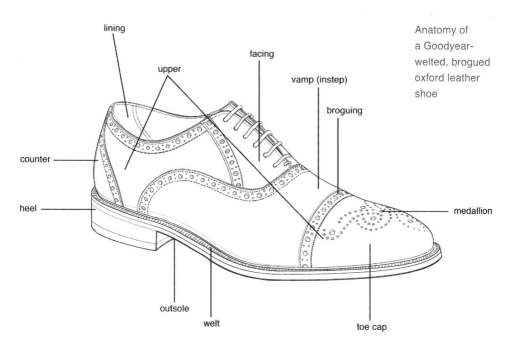

Anatomy of a Goodyear-welted, brogued oxford leather shoe

although not always, corresponds to quality. And a minimum exists, below which quality just can't be found because of the fundamental costs of materials, design, and construction.

As a customer, how can you know whether that is the reason for a high price tag? Truth is, it's up to you to do the research. Ask the seller plenty of questions and find out what you can about the maker. What I've learned to look for is a shoemaker who is transparent about where their shoes are made, what processes they use, and which tanneries they source their leathers from. This often means, in my experience, smaller European brands or heritage makers.

> Avoid designer shoes from fashion labels: they are notorious for cutting corners when it comes to quality in order to cover their marketing and licensing budgets.

As hard as it may be to believe, investing in quality can actually save you money. Here's my experience. A number of years ago I bought a pair of shoes for around $100. They had low-quality leather uppers, a synthetic liner, and glued-on rubber soles. No matter how much I took care of the uppers, they never took a polish well, and the shoes lost what little shape they had in just a few months. After a year the lining started to fray and come apart. After two years the soles began to wear thin and could not be replaced. There was nothing I could do but reluctantly throw them away.

On the other hand, I have a pair of mid-quality shoes that cost around $500. They are made completely of leather that, while not the highest grade, is of good quality. The front half of the sole has been replaced once (for a cost of around $50), and they are now almost ten years old. If, in the next ten years, I were to have them completely re-soled for approximately $200, that would put their per-year cost at $37.50. The cheaper shoes? More, at $50 a year. And, of course, along the way the more expensive shoes look and feel much, much better. In a sense, you are pro-rating the cost of your shoes: it isn't about the upfront cost, but how that cost is spread out over the life of the shoes. Longer life, lower year-by-year cost — not to mention, a better experience over that time of both fit and style.

Consider, as well, the added environmental benefit: since I'm not throwing the shoes away and replacing them every year or so, I'm producing much less waste over the lifetime of the shoes. So the first lesson is not so much about shoes but about spending. You can change your habits from a lot of small purchases to fewer, larger purchases.

But investing in quality is also about appreciating good things. Yes, that includes exceptional craft and materials that will give you a feeling of satisfaction every time you wear the items. For me, however, quality is also about beauty. There is something so unique, so beautiful, about how fine shoes are able to combine function and aesthetics. Having something in your life that is aesthetically beautiful — which could be because of the leather, the shape of the shoe, the details in the finishing, or all three — nourishes you in ways I think we undervalue. If the world around us is full of ugly things, we can't help but feel that the world itself is ugly. Fill our lives with beautiful things, and we believe the world is just that much more beautiful. Neither is a completely true reflection of reality, of course, but I prefer to choose positivity over negativity.

What Makes a Shoe a Shoe

When I grew up, like many people I called leather shoes "dress shoes." Partially this is because I only wore my leather shoes to church, with my ill-fitting polyester suit (vivid detail about that in the "Two-Piece Suits" section). It was also because we as a society don't really know what "dress" is anymore. Technically and historically, a "dress shoe" is any footwear you wear with black or white tie, such as patent leather oxfords or opera slippers. What I'm talking about in this chapter is any style of all-leather shoe meant to be worn with anything — anything *except* formal dress on one end and for playing sports on the other. Within that range, however, are a multitude of options. But before we look at the outside, the style of a shoe, we need to start with the inside, what makes a shoe a shoe. And that begins with the last.

LASTS

Typically made of wood or plastic, a last looks like a foot without toes and is the shape around which leather is stretched to give the shoe its shape and silhouette (not to be confused with shoe trees, which help maintain shoes in good condition, see "Caring for Your Wardrobe"). All shoes made of leather are constructed on lasts, which are mass produced at standard sizes. Lasts can also be custom-made and shaped, based on your measurements, for custom shoes. A mass-market or custom last can be rounded or pointy toed, and the way the shoe will shape around the instep, the volume of the shoe, and even the shape of the heel are determined by the last.

Traditional
wooden
shoe lasts

Understanding lasts will liberate you from the shackles of shoe sizes. I grew up thinking my shoe size was 10.5 wide. It turns out, the situation is more complicated than that. First of all, my left foot is slightly longer than my right (for the vast majority of people, one foot is a different size than the other). However, my right foot splays more than my left when walking. So which one is really bigger? I also have a high instep (the part of your foot right under the laces). All of this means that I used to buy shoes that were too big, trying to compensate for all my idiosyncrasies, so that they would feel "comfortable." This really meant I was striving to not feel the shoes at all. The lasts that all those poor-quality shoes were built upon were generous: wide and voluminous. Even though they measured 10.5

inches long, the space inside the shoe was enough to accommodate a range of foot sizes, from medium to wide width. Which meant they fit most people badly and fit no one perfectly.

Then I discovered not only that shoes are built on lasts but also that lasts come in so many shapes, depending on the maker. And I realized that if I found the right maker using just the right shaped last for me, I could have the length I needed plus the height in my instep, but in a shoe that hugged my ankles and held my toes firm. However, finding the right last means trying a variety of shoes from a variety of makers. But honestly, that is part of the fun. With every shoe you try on, you learn more about yourself and about shoes.

MATERIALS

The truth is, even "all-leather" shoes do have other materials in them. There might be cork in the sole, metal in the shank, or rubber covering the bottom of the sole. What is key is that the entire upper (the "outside" of the top of the shoe), the lining (the inside), and the sole (including the heel) should be made of leather. That said, there's leather, and then there's leather.

You may have seen the term "genuine leather" and assumed it meant high quality. Sadly, that assumption is wrong. Genuine leather is a blanket term for various types of low-grade, low-quality leathers that are sometimes even reconstituted from smaller pieces. "Genuine leather" is best avoided. Finding good leather shoes is not as simple as a label.

The best leather for shoes is "full grain," but within that category many, many options form a sliding scale of quality. So while looking for full grain is a good starting point, it is not a guarantee of quality. For instance, many tanneries offer different grades of quality within their full grain range. The quality can even depend on which part of the hide the leather is from. And then there is the question of tanning: what method was used (vegetable, chrome, etc.) as well as the company's history and technical skill. Good-quality leather can be tanned poorly.

The "shank" is shaped like a small shoehorn and gives the sole support. It can be made of metal, wood, plastic, or other materials. Metal or wood is best for support and durability. The "heel counter" sits inside the back of the shoe to give your heel support. Best when made of leather, it might also be plastic or paper.

I'm not suggesting you research every single tannery that every single shoemaker might use. But I do think you need to be aware of the challenges when selecting leather so that you aren't easily hoodwinked. Thankfully, there are some guidelines to help you navigate this sea of options.

If the shoe is made with full grain European calf leather, you are in the right zone — and I stipulate European because of the strict regulations there around the tanning of leather. You see, leather is an extremely hazardous and polluting material to produce. But if you are using European full grain leather, you can be relatively sure that

Here's a good test when buying shoes: If the salesperson cannot tell you anything about the leather used in the shoes they are selling, or how they were welted, take your business elsewhere.

the leather was a by-product of the food industry and that the tanning was done to some of the most stringent environmental standards in the world. It's not perfect, but of all the options, this kind of leather is perhaps the best you can do environmentally (including, I would argue, artificial leather, which is usually made of polyurethane, i.e., petroleum). European tanneries also have, on average, a longer history, which suggests more knowledge and therefore a better tanning process. They are more likely, though not guaranteed, to source better raw materials. Keep in mind, as well, that if properly cared for (see "Caring for Your Wardrobe"), quality leather shoes will last well over a decade, thus reducing their total footprint.

CONSTRUCTION

The traditional method of making a pair of leather shoes is an exercise in hidden architecture. There is so much more to a shoe than meets the eye. You don't need to spend months studying shoemaking to understand the basics of good construction that lead to quality footwear. That said, there are some things to be aware of.

A basic leather shoe is constructed of these parts: the upper (outside of the shoe), the liner (the inside), the insole (the part your foot comes in contact with), the outsole (the part the ground comes in contact with), and the heel. Pretty much every shoe, of every quality, requires glue at some point in construction, but it is how the outsole is connected to the insole that matters. This part should never be glued if you want a shoe that will last a long time and be repairable. How the outsole is stitched to the insole can be a matter of price but not necessarily quality. The most expensive and time-consuming method is hand-welting, where the sole is attached with a continuous hand applied stitch. While this is usually done only on high-quality shoes, in some cases shoes that are hand-welted may be otherwise poorly lasted or finished.

Goodyear welting is a mechanical process that is difficult to master and requires an investment in training, skill, and machinery. The "Goodyear Welting Machine," patented by Charles Goodyear Jr., the son of the vulcanized rubber inventor, industrialized the making of shoes in the nineteenth century by mechanizing the process of attaching the upper and insole to the outsole. They are attached separately, which means Goodyear shoes can be re-soled relatively easily, by simply replacing the outsole. But a Goodyear welt may be used on a shoe made with lower-quality leather, so it alone is not a guarantee of overall quality.

And finally there is Blake stitching, another method named after a machine. Blake stitching produces a slim, sleek sole by stitching the outsole, insole, and upper at once. Blake welting is less expensive to produce than Goodyear but harder to re-sole, and it can't be re-soled as many times. That said, plenty of high-quality shoes are Blake stitched.

Quality Check

When you are holding a pair of shoes in your hands, look for some specific features to help you identify quality. First, look closely at the leather, but don't let shine fool you. Poor-quality leather can be plasticized to make it look shiny. Instead, look for a subtle grain and a lustre that is neither shiny nor dull. Second, look at the stitching around the upper to see if it is smooth, consistent, and even. Check that the stitching is real: many companies use fake stitching to give the appearance of welting when, in fact, the shoes are glued together. Third, look at the lining: if it has a clean, even stitch all the way around, that's a sign that extra care was probably taken during the rest of the shoemaking process. Fourth, if the shoe has a hard structure around the heel (the counter) and the toecap, can you push your thumb into it? If so, a cheaper plastic or paper stiffener was probably used and the shoes should be avoided.

You may occasionally come across a claim of "handmade" shoes. There is really no such thing. And no reason to believe that even if there were, they would automatically be of better quality. There might be a lot of handwork involved in the making of a shoe — in the lasting, welting, and finishing — but there is always machine work, usually in stitching the upper, and hand work does not guarantee quality.

So while you should look for a welted shoe — one where the sole is stitched and not glued, quality comes from how a number of factors work together. These include what type of construction is used, how the sole is welted, where the factory is located (again, Europe usually means higher environmental and working standards), and how many shoes the factory produces (often the fewer the better). And, of course, the quality of leather.

Fit

I grew up misunderstanding how a shoe should fit. Whenever we were shopping for shoes, my mother would judge their suitability based on the amount of space in front of my big toe. A bit of space meant a perfect fit, no space meant a bad fit. In her defence, I was a growing boy and she was probably just worried about replacing my shoes every few months. But, of course, that toe-space measurement says nothing about the rest of your foot. Not to mention that, in my experience, having your toes completely free and easy is not the ideal starting point to a shoe's fit.

There are a number of things I look for in fit, and this is easily the most complex and personal of the decisions you have to make when buying shoes. However, some lessons I've learned have served me well.

The first is that leather shoes should be tight when new. Not painful, but not roomy. Your foot should be held firm, as if someone is gripping your foot but not squeezing it. When you walk, your toes should have minimal movement, but not so little that you feel pain. Your heel should be cupped so well that it does not move up and down as you walk. And the facings (where the laces are threaded on oxfords and derbies) should just about meet. If doing up the shoes means the facings push against each other, then there is too much room in the instep. If there is a huge gap, not enough room.

As you wear the shoes, the leather will soften up just enough to provide real comfort: a firm but not constricting hold of your foot. This breaking-in period can take, in my experience, up to twenty-four hours of wear. A friend even suggests wearing new shoes around the house at first, for a couple of hours at a time. This way, eventually, the upper and the insole will contour and shape to your foot thanks to the heat and humidity of wear.

If your shoes are off-the-rack, there is a good chance that no matter how much research you do, how many pairs you try, how judicious you are in purchasing, the fit will not be quite right. Don't worry: it's not you; it's the shoes. No two feet are the same, even on the same person, so how could a pair of ready-made shoes fit everyone just right? Instead, you can make a number of adjustments for a better fit. If the volume of the shoe feels slightly too large, you can decrease a half size with an added insole. However, this can have the effect of pushing your foot up and out of the shoe. To counter this, add a pad to the underside of the shoe's tongue. This also helps if your foot is slipping in the heel a bit. I find this much more effective than heel grips.

Style

The options for leather shoes are almost limitless. All that choice can be daunting, so let's start big picture with some basic shoe types, from formal to casual:

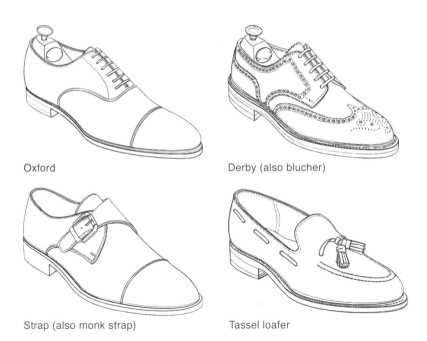

Oxford

Derby (also blucher)

Strap (also monk strap)

Tassel loafer

OXFORD The most formal shoe style, the oxford is identified by its closed lacing, which means the part of the upper with the lace holes is connected, as if all one piece, to the rest of the upper.

DERBY/BLUCHER A style that can be both formal and casual, the derby (sometimes known as "blucher" in America) is identified by open lacing. Unlike an oxford, the facing that holds the lacing holes is stitched on top of the upper.

STRAP A strap shoe is a more casual style, sometimes with one, two, or more straps, and sometimes referred to as "monk strap." Straps are clearly identified by the presence of metal buckles instead of laces.

LOAFER The most casual of leather shoes, some styles of loafers, such as tassel and penny loafer, can be worn in more formal settings, even with suits. Others, like moccasins and driving loafers, best suit casual wear.

Within each of those categories are numerous options. For instance, some shoes can have broguing, or rows and patterns of holes in the leather. These traditionally make the shoes more casual and can be added to any of the styles listed above. At the other end of the scale is a wholecut, where the entire upper is made of one piece of leather. This is a style used on oxfords because of the integrated facing, and it can make the shoes seem more formal.

So, how do you even get started selecting a shoe style? Much of the choice is personal preference, doing the work of self-discovery to determine if loafers are more your thing than oxfords. But you must also consider the rest of your wardrobe, the climate you live in, and your day-to-day activities.

A hyper-mini guide to shoe formality: the simpler the shoe (oxford, wholecut), the more formal; the more complicated (pattern, colour, broguing), the more casual.

Colour

You're either a funky-shoe guy or you're not. Because once you start down that road, the rest of your wardrobe has to live up to the promise loudly proclaimed by your red, yellow, or blue shoes. I sit solidly on the non-funky side.

I'll admit I toyed with colour at one point. When I got my first pair of custom shoes, *because I could do anything*, I decided on two-tone oxfords. While I thought I was being subtle with a mid-brown suede facing and lighter-brown upper, the shoes felt so loud, I rarely wore them. Which is a shame because being custom-made, and made expertly, they fit extremely well. What I should have done sounds like a boring choice: dark-brown oxfords. But if I had, I would have worn them much, much more often. And that's the point of a great pair of shoes: wearing them, not owning them. (This is also how menswear generally differs from women's fashion: men's clothing is traditionally versatile and interchangeable, not unique, one-off pieces meant to be worn only a couple of times a year, if that.)

It was a lesson I brought to the rest of my shoe wardrobe. Since I'm trying to move more and more toward subtlety in my clothing, and since shoes are the visual foundation of your outfit, each pair I buy is more conservative. Mid- to dark brown. They harmonize with every shade of the trousers I wear. Brown is more visually interesting than black (and less formal) while not as attention-grabbing as other colours. Apologies to my funky-footed friends, but nothing does it for me quite like a well-made pair of tassel loafers in mid-brown with a slight polish and a bit of burnishing at the toe. (Burnishing is when you use a dark cream or polish at the toe to create a subtle darker patina over time).

My Own Shoe Wardrobe

Experimenting with different styles of shoes until you find what works for you can be expensive. But once you pass through that process, you will probably establish a look that takes you through many decades of your life. I knew early on that I liked simple brown leather shoes. I was drawn to the rakishness of double monks and tried a pair for a few months only to find that they stood out a bit too much for me. Selling them second-hand was a way to recoup at least some of my cost. The rest I chalked up to learning an important lesson about my own sense of style.

I learned I liked simplicity and understatement but also that just because a pair of shoes looks lovely doesn't mean I will like

Suede Shoes

Suede occupies an interesting middle ground of formality. Its napped finish definitely makes a shoe more casual, but it does so with personality. Nothing expresses relaxed elegance more to me than mid-brown suede loafers. However, some people have an aversion to suede. Some think that suede is more delicate and harder to care for than calf leather, while in fact the opposite is true (see "Caring for Your Wardrobe"). And per-haps there is a holdover from prejudices of the early twentieth century. On a trip to America in the 1920s, the Prince of Wales (later the Duke of Windsor) was warned that suede shoes were worn only by homosexuals. He didn't wear suede for the rest of his trip. I'm not saying that suede is still associated with homosexuality, but it does denote a love and concern for dressing still con-sidered, by many, to be unmanly. This is both ri-diculous and unfortunate, cutting us off from an entire range of expression and beauty.

It is important to have a few pairs of shoes, and not for reasons of vanity. Okay, not *completely* for reasons of vanity. Don't wear the same pair of shoes two days in a row. Sweat is the biggest factor in wearing down your shoes, and a day's rest will give them time to dry out and recover from a punishing day on your feet, helping them last much, much longer.

the way they look on my feet. I learned to consider the rest of my wardrobe before buying shoes: am I mostly formal or casual, colourful or toned down? And to always consider how I live my life: city or country, mostly on my feet or seated, climate and temperature, etc.

Further to the latter, I separate my shoes into two seasons: fall/winter and spring/summer. And I try to have at least one pair of shoes for each type of occasion in each season, from casual to formal.

For fall/winter, I stick to leather shoes in various shades of brown, which again goes with practically everything (except black tie, for which I have a pair of black patent leather oxfords). For more casual clothes — like chinos and flannel trousers — I have a pair of longwing brogues (brogues are any style of leather shoe, oxford or derby, adorned with perforated patterns) as well as a pair of country boots. The boots are great when it's snowy but I still want to look sharp. If I'm headed somewhere boots would be out of place, I have galoshes shaped like boots that protect my oxfords perfectly. Between casual and formal are my split-toed derbies and suede shoes. And then my dressiest are two pairs of oxfords in different shades of brown. This is probably twice as many shoes as I really need, but the variety, quality, and care I put into them means I won't need new shoes for decades to come.

My spring/summer shoe wardrobe is more casual. While I always keep one pair of darker-brown oxfords on hand in case of a business meeting or more formal event, I prefer loafers for day-to-day wear. My darker-brown suede Belgian loafers are a way to add a relaxed touch to a more formal outfit, or a touch of elegance to a more casual look. I have mid-brown penny and tassel loafers that look great with cotton and linen chinos, and suede moccasins for even more casual outfits. Even on the hottest, most humid days, I find loafers supremely comfortable thanks to an important discovery I made a few years ago: terry cloth inserts. When going barefoot, instead of no-show socks, I prefer cloth inserts. They are cushioned and comfortable, absorb sweat, and can easily be lifted out of the shoe and washed.

Quality over Quantity

Fundamentally, the lesson you can learn from building a shoe wardrobe is a shift in thinking away from quantity (lots of cheap shoes) to quality (one or two pairs of truly well-made shoes). And that is an investment in craftspeople, tradition, beauty, and a more meaningful relationship with our clothes.

Shirts

The shirt is a triumph of modern life, like the automobile or the web. It is easy to put on and take off, quick to wash and easy to store. Plus, shirts look great. A man should own as many shirts as he wishes — the more the better.

— Luciano Barbera

The garment you're probably wearing right now — with a collar, cuffs, and with buttons up the front — was originally underwear. When the contemporary shirt was first created by Charvet in Paris in the early nineteenth century, most of it was covered up. High-buttoning waistcoats and jackets obscured everything but the cuffs and collars, which is one reason these two elements have remained so important and defining in a shirt's design: originally, they were all you could see.

In the twentieth century, starting with the casual revolution that came after the First World War, the shirt was liberated from behind ounces of heavy cloth to become outerwear in its own right. And yet, despite all the changes from the original pullover starched collar shirt to the garment we know today, it is still beholden to its sartorial history. The collar, for instance, was created to hold and frame a tie or cravat, though sadly men rarely wear any silk at the neck anymore. Cuffs and collars used to be detachable because washing was a much bigger chore and those parts of the shirt were more likely to get dirty or worn. You would remove them (well, okay, your valet would remove them), boil out the starch, wash them, starch them back up, and reattach them to the shirt. The body itself wasn't washed as often. Thankfully, today shirt washing is as easy as the permanent-press cycle in a washing machine (although some handwashing is still a good idea; see "Caring for Your Wardrobe"). Despite those changes, history is the reason we have so many options when it comes to cuffs and collars.

Not only have shirt designs and how we wear them gone through a transformation in the last hundred years, but also our concept of fit. In the past, when so little of the shirt was seen, the sleeves and body could be as loose and blousy as desired, for maximum comfort and movement. Now that shirts are worn as outerwear, many men want them to fit like jackets: tapered and close to the body. Sadly, though, this means many contemporary "slim fit" shirts only look good — or even function — if you are impossibly svelte and never planning to sit down or move your arms. If you do, the fabric and buttons strain to the point of bursting.

You see, a shirt isn't built like a jacket, which, thanks to its layers of padding and extra cloth, can be close to the body and still functional. In a shirt, there are no layers and no padding; the fabric is different and lighter and, thus, can't be shaped and pressed into three dimensions the same way. In fact, a shirt has no shape other than your own.

I believe that understanding history is key to learning how to select and build your own wardrobe of shirts (and every other garment in this book). This starts with deciding whether the shirt will be worn as background (under a jacket or knitwear) or foreground (your primary outerwear without a jacket).

Off-the-Rack versus Custom

There are so many options when it comes to what type and style of shirt you want, and even where to get it. A case can be made for both custom-made and off-the-rack shirts, and it comes down to the quality on offer, your individual needs, and your budget. One is not necessarily better than the other. Ready-made shirts are available at almost all price points and qualities of manufacturing. They are easy to buy because you can simply try one on to determine if the fit and style are to your liking (taking into consideration the guidance provided below). And so off-the-rack will work best for many men. But not all.

I choose to go the custom route not because I'm physically un-usual but because I am sartorially obsessive (surprise, surprise). I love building a connection to my clothing from the ground up, choosing everything from the shirt's fabric, to all the features, to as good a fit as possible. And from made to order, through made to measure, and finally to bespoke, the options are almost endless. In a sense, you are starting from scratch, able to choose from all the features and elements and fabrics discussed in this chapter to create your own unique shirt, crafted by a shirtmaker to your exact specifications. But again, if that maker isn't top notch or if you and the maker don't see eye to eye, cus-tom won't necessarily produce a better garment than one off-the-rack.

Regardless of whether you go custom or ready-made, there are a number of key factors you need to understand before building a shirt wardrobe: fabric types, colours and patterns, collar styles, other shirt features like cuffs and buttons, as well as construction and fit.

Fabric

I'm the kind of guy who's really put off when a word is misused. I know, I know, there are more important things in the world to get worked up about, but sometimes I can't help sweating the small stuff. Small stuff like "shirting." This term refers to the fabric used in the making of shirts. But the word has become, in the world of marketing, a flashy, tailor-sounding stand-in for the more prosaic word "shirts." Please don't use it that way. Shirts are shirts. And shirt fabric is a whole other world.

The Burn Test

To determine if a fabric is blended with polyester, you can do the burn test — if the bulk fabric store you're in is okay with your lighting things on fire. Burn just a tiny corner of the fabric: if it's pure cotton, it smells like burning paper and leaves a soft grey or black ash; if it's a poly-blend, it smells like burning chemicals and feels hard and beaded when extinguished.

While fabric might not be the first thing you think about when choosing a shirt — collar shape, colour, and pattern are probably the first things that draw your eye — shirting has a profound impact on a shirt's look and longevity. But I will warn you, the array of fabric types, plies, thread counts, and so on seems endless. In this chapter, I will focus on the most common, the ones you're most likely to run into, and the ones that matter most when looking for quality. This applies to every type of shirt because the first thing I want you to consider is the fabric, especially if the shirt is off-the-rack.

Without question, your shirts should be 100 percent natural fibres, cotton being the most popular. I once made the mistake of buying a shirt that was a blend of cotton and polyester. I was in a rush and I temporarily lowered my standards. The fabric felt slicker than it should have and started pilling after just a few washes. It gives off a chemical smell when ironed and, worst of all, doesn't breathe as well as 100 percent cotton.

> Even though non-iron shirts may be 100 percent cotton, they have been chemically treated to retain their shape. See page 201 in "Caring for Your Wardrobe" for the full, gruesome story.

Natural fabrics breathe, wash well, and last if properly taken care of (see "Caring for Your Wardrobe"). But "100 percent cotton" isn't that simple to define. You'll typically find three types of cotton used in the highest quality shirtings: Egyptian, Sea Island, and Pima (sometimes labelled "Supima"). The thing is, those names get abused by less scrupulous sellers. Egyptian cotton is defined by extra-long fibres (which produce finer, stronger yarn), but it is sometimes mixed with poor-quality, short-fibre cotton. Sea Island, meanwhile, is extremely rare, expensive, and hard to come by. While these labels are a good start, you'll have to learn to trust your hand to determine quality: does the shirting feel good to the touch? Personally, I like shirting that is soft yet firm and not rough (unless it is a pure linen or casual oxford). For dressier shirts, I want the fabric to be smooth and sturdy without feeling like it's stiff or made of plastic. It should have a lustre that isn't shiny.

Other natural fabrics are used for shirting, but the one I recommend apart from cotton is linen. When it comes to warm-weather wear, nothing beats linen: it feels light on the body, it wicks away sweat, and its open weave allows cooling air to pass easily to your skin. But there are trade-offs to these benefits. First, the sweat wicking can mean that linen gets smelly faster. Second, the open weave of linen can mean harmful rays get through and burn your skin. A cotton T-shirt worn underneath is my solution to that problem. Third, and this is really a style question, linen famously wrinkles. But I don't see that as a trade-off; in fact, it's one of linen's stylish traits. If you're wearing linen, it's probably stinking hot. And if it's stinking hot and you can wear linen, you're probably in a casual environment. And nothing emotes stylish nonchalance like rumpled linen. If, however, I want something not quite so schlubby, I'll go for shirting in a linen/cotton blend: it tends to hold its shape better while still remaining relatively light and airy.

PLY AND THREAD COUNT

Shirting has a lot of numbers associated with it. "Ply" is the number of yarns used in a fabric's thread. There is either a single ply, or when two threads are wound tightly around each other, a double or "two-ply." The latter produces a more durable and finer fabric and is therefore preferable. Another common number relating to shirt fabrics is thread count, which should more correctly be called "yarn count." Thread count is literally the number of yarns per linear inch in a fabric; the higher the number, the more yarns, and the tighter the weave. This number can range from 80 on the low end to 220 on the high. Closely connected to the thread count is the yarn number, which refers to the thickness of the individual yarns; they run from "24s" at the coarse end to "200s" at the thinnest. For instance, a fabric with a high thread count most likely uses a thin yarn (so they can all be fit in).

All of these numbers can be overwhelming and, in truth, they are not a surefire guide to quality. In other words, while two-ply is a must, simply looking for shirting that is 150/2 (thread count/ply) does not guarantee excellent cloth. It is better to understand that the higher the count, the thinner and smoother the cloth. Fabric quality really comes down to a combination of cotton type, who milled it, and ply. The thread and yarn counts matter if you want a finer or rougher weave, but not necessarily a better shirting.

WEAVES

Once you get past the numbers, prepare yourself for another barrage of choices: fabric weaves. Thankfully, most can be broken down into a few categories from the dressiest to the most casual: broadcloth, oxford, and twill.

BROADCLOTH The vast majority of dress shirting is made with the broadcloth weave, which is also referred to as poplin, essentially the same thing. In its basic form, it is the simplest of weaves: one thread in the weft (horizontal) passing over one thread in the warp (vertical), then under and over and under and over, and so on. This produces a smooth, strong, and durable cloth that can also be lightweight, thus perfect for spring and summer.

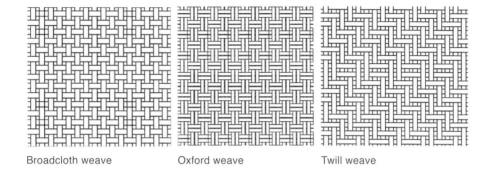

Broadcloth weave   Oxford weave   Twill weave

OXFORD Another common weave is oxford, which is so closely related to pinpoint weave and basket weave that I'll group them together. Oxford cloth can be woven quite tightly or loosely, resulting in a dressy or rustic finish. The weave is achieved by a number of weft threads going over and under an equal number of warp threads, resulting in a basket pattern. They are often woven in solid colours, but sometimes oxfords are woven of two colours: the main colour of the shirt (such as blue) and white — one in the weft, one in the warp — creating a tiny checkerboard pattern.

TWILL Well suited for fall and winter shirting, twill includes the variations of gabardine, cavalry, and herringbone. Twill is created by a weft passing over a number of warp threads then under only one before going over a number of threads again. The following row of weft threads does the same, but shifted over by one. This produces a diagonal ribbing effect in a cloth that is the most durable of all the variations.

All of these names and numbers come down to a simple truth. The rougher the fabric, the more casual; the smoother, the more formal. I have a three-way split in my closet: a few fine broadcloth shirts in white and blue for dressing up; a few loosely woven oxfords and linens for casual wear; and then the majority, a collection of twills or finer oxfords that I can wear with or without a tie.

Personally, I'm a big fan of oxford cloth. A heavy, rough blue oxford almost looks and feels like denim but is fine enough to wear with a tie. It's everything I want my clothing to be: casual or dressy, depending on how I wear it. The sturdiness of the fabric makes me feel assured and confident, and I could go the rest of my life wearing no other button-down shirt. What jeans are to most people an oxford cloth button-down is to me. Even the way the collars and cuffs start to fray after a few years of wear is, I find, more satisfying and rakish than any kind of denim fade.

COLOUR AND PATTERN

Someone who knows far more about colour theory would probably be able to figure this out, but the best shirt colour for almost all men is blue. It compliments any skin tone as well as almost any other part of an outfit, be it a jacket, trousers, or a sweater. The majority of my shirts are blue and solid blue at that. They are almost all mid- to light blues and there is a reason behind that choice.

In simple terms, the darker the colour or the bigger the pattern, the more casual the shirt. A plain white shirt, therefore, is the most formal. Mid- to light blues are the most versatile and can be worn casually or with more dressy outfits. The more colours and patterns in a shirt, the more difficult it will be to combine it with other elements. Shirts with more colours or patterns are probably best worn with plain trousers and no jacket. I choose plain mid-blues for my shirts because I can wear them with almost anything, from dressy to casual. The problem with "statement" shirts that have really pronounced colours or patterns is that I almost never wear them. Not only are they readily identifiable ("Hey, Pedro's wearing *that* shirt again!"), but I'd also rather make my own statements.

One classic style of shirt that combines different colours and is considered dressy, not casual, is the contrast collar and cuffs shirt — think Gordon Gekko in the movie *Wall Street*. These shirts originated when collar and cuffs would wear down but the rest of a shirt was still in good condition, so a tailor would just replace the necessary elements. Since finding the exact shirting would be almost impossible (not to mention that years of wear and laundering would have faded the shirt colour slightly), tailors would instead use white for the collar and cuffs. As these shirts were mostly worn by businessmen throughout the twentieth century, the look has become associated with office culture and formality. Also, contrast collar and cuffs shirts have long been available pre-made and off-the-rack. I have only ever owned one contrast shirt, and I rarely wore it; it's a style that feels too laden with historical associations to work for me. Even when I'm dressed up, I prefer to be understated.

Collar Style

The first time I visited Italy, I remember looking out my taxi window as we moved slowly through the streets of Milan. We stopped at a red light and I noticed a man on a second-floor balcony smoking a cigarette. What first caught my eye was not his flowing hair, or his nonchalantly rolled up sleeves, or even all the buttons he'd undone on his shirt for maximum *heavage*. It was the roll of his button-down collar. The collar itself was long, and that, combined with the placement of the buttons, gave his collar a full, long S roll. I didn't think it was ostentatious or macho (like his heavage). But it was sensual. And liberating. Here was a man confident enough in himself, I thought, to boldly express this side of his masculinity.

Men's collars used to be much longer. In the 1930s the California collar extended five inches down a man's chest. Today, I often see collars on fashionable shirts that are barely two inches. And this isn't just about fashion. For the last few decades shirt collars have reflected, I think, a discomfort some North American and Northern European men have with sensuality. Again, this could be tied to distrust of manly ostentation. But it also speaks to a deep-seated prudishness — which is strange in a self-proclaimed "liberated" society.

Whether you want long collar points or not, the collar of your shirt will have the biggest impact of any feature because of its prominence and how it frames your face. It forms a sort of inverted triangle (especially when combined with a tie) that points straight up to your face, where you want to encourage people to look.

The Button-Down

Collars were first buttoned at the corner to shirt fronts by British polo players around the turn of the last century, in an attempt to keep them from flopping around during games. One of the Brooks Brothers saw this and quite liked it — and this is one reason their button-downs are still called "Polo shirts" to this day. But while the button-down began as a sports shirt, fashion-conscious college kids in the 1920s and 30s began pairing button-downs with more formal clothing — like jackets and even suits — which some Brits still frown on today. So why do most people think of button-downs as conservative and, well, *buttoned-down*? Well, those college kids went on to become businessmen in the 1950s and 60s and kept wearing their button-downs, along with their grey flannel suits. I prefer to return to the shirt's original iteration, not for playing polo (which I've never done) but as a rakish mixing of casual and formal.

There is an accepted belief that collar shape corresponds to face shape, in that slender, point collars help narrow a wide face, and spread collars balance a narrow face. I have never found this to be true in practice, maybe because we rarely see a face and collar in isolation; other elements are always at play. Or maybe because it

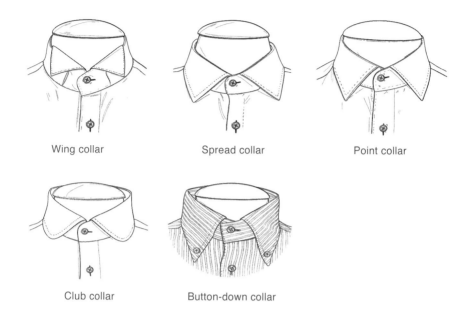

Wing collar   Spread collar   Point collar

Club collar   Button-down collar

isn't that simple. My face, for example, is on the narrow side of oval, yet I seem to be able to wear all collar types without looking like a basketball or Beaker from *The Muppet Show*.

From formal to casual, these are the main types of shirt collars: wing, spread, point, club, and button-down. Once you've decided on the type of collar you prefer but before you begin the process of looking for a shirt, make sure to have your neck measured properly. The measuring tape should be wrapped around your neck just below the Adam's apple, with two fingers placed inside the tape. That measurement is the starting point for picking any shirt because that is how shirtmakers usually define their shirt sizes. When you try on

Collars and Tie Knots

There is only one tie knot I use and, therefore, recommend: the four-in-hand. It is simple, elegant, and asymmetrical. Serious without being too serious. The thickness of your tie will dictate the thickness of the resulting knot. Now, I don't subscribe to the idea that wide, spread collars demand wide tie knots and vice versa. While I do think a thin tie knot looks even smaller with a spread collar, there is no need to resort to the double Windsor knot. Ever. Instead, simply use a double four-in-hand (the fabric is initially looped around twice, making the knot wider). I find the double Windsor too large and lacking in subtlety and personality. Even the Duke of Windsor didn't use one; his ties just had a thicker lining, so his knots were larger, yes, but with the asymmetric rakishness of the four-in-hand.

a shirt, always do up the top button, even if you never intend to wear a tie. The collar needs to be fitted, such that your neck is not floating around in empty space like a twelve-year-old dressed for a wedding. But it also needs to be comfortable so that you won't feel like murdering someone after wearing it all day long.

Historically, collars were starched until they were as stiff as boards. This fit in with Victorian ideals of dress, which were equally stiff and regimented. But the twentieth century brought casualness to all forms of dress, and the shirt collar was one of the first things affected. The Duke of Windsor turned the world of menswear upside down when he famously wore a turndown, soft collar with his tuxedo. He was the original punk rocker. By this point, the horse had left the barn and soft collars were here to stay. In fact, the first button-down collars from Brooks Brothers had no lining inside of them whatsoever and were not at all starched, so the collars were as soft and formless as the rest of the shirt. And while this has the effect of casual nonchalance, some men still prefer a bit more stiffness to their collars. Many collars today have a lining, usually fused to the outer side, to give the collar sturdiness and to make it easier to press. Nothing wrong with that, if you like the look. Collars can also be made firmer with collar stays, small slits of metal, mother-of-pearl or plastic that slip into the underside of collars, near the tips. I always purchase shirts with removable stays so that I can decide, each time I wear the shirt, if I prefer the collar stiff or a bit softer.

Another subtlety of collar construction to be aware of is collar band height. The collar band is the part of the shirt that wraps around your neck and to which the collar attaches. While most off-the-rack shirts come in a standard collar height of about an inch, some brands and all custom makers have the option of a slightly higher or shorter collar band. This is a great choice if you have a shorter or longer neck. My neck is neither on the long nor short side, but since I am tall, I can accommodate a slightly taller band.

Other Shirt Features

Beyond the collar, there are a number of other features that greatly affect the look of a shirt. In general, the basic rule is this: the more features, the more casual a shirt will look. Further, it looks odd to mix casual with formal within a single garment. For example, adding two flapped, buttoned pockets to a dressy spread collar shirt. I always think about the history and associations of the features before making a purchase or ordering a custom shirt.

POCKETS

It is traditional for shirts to have a single, open pocket over the left breast. Formal shirts do not have any pockets — you are not supposed to be carrying around the detritus of daily life in formal attire — so a lack of pockets makes a shirt look dressier. The more intricate a pocket's design, however, such as added pleats, flaps, and buttons, the more casual the overall shirt will look.

The Duke of Windsor

Formerly the Prince of Wales, briefly the uncrowned King of England, Edward, Duke of Windsor, will be forever shrouded in a cloud of controversy. However, what cannot be denied is the Duke's influence on menswear. Sartorially, his focus on comfort liberated men in the Western world from frock coats and starched collars. He cemented items of country and sportswear — cuffed trousers, Fair Isle sweaters, tweed everything — as city wear. As the most photographed man of the early twentieth century, he was the world's first male fashion influencer: men were said to have standing orders with their tailors to replicate anything he was seen wearing. He was a beacon for modern style in an era still ensconced in Victorian and Edwardian values. As menswear historian and writer G. Bruce Boyer says, "He was the brightest of the Bright Young Things, slim and easygoing, given to jazz and slang, night clubs and open convertibles. He set a tone and mood for his time that is still with us today."

PLACKETS

The same logic applies to plackets, the area that runs down the front of the shirt where the buttons are threaded through. There are typically only three styles of front plackets. The most common, usually known as a classic or standard placket, is stitched on both sides, creating what looks like a strip of fabric down the front of the shirt. Despite being the most common, this is also the most casual style of placket due to the extra stitching. A dressier style is the French front, on which the fabric isn't folded over and stitched. The placket is clean and unadorned, with only buttonholes interrupting the front of the shirt. The most formal style is the covered placket, where the buttons are buttoned to a strip of fabric behind the placket, leaving the front of the shirt completely uninterrupted. Almost all of my shirts have classic plackets as they are the most versatile.

You'll also find a placket on the sleeve of a shirt (also called a "gauntlet"). Other than the button on the cuff, this placket usually has a single small button halfway along. I hate that button.

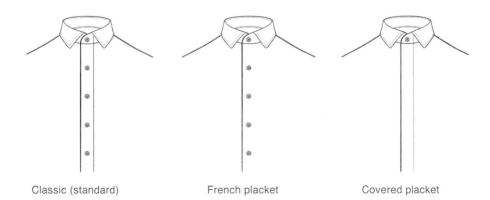

Classic (standard)   French placket   Covered placket

Darts, most often used on the fronts of sport jackets, are used for shaping a garment. A slit is made down the length of the fabric, and when sewn back together, some of that fabric is tucked into a seam or removed, making the garment slightly tighter where the dart is (for example, at the waist).

When I'm putting on or taking off a shirt, it seems like a needless bit of excess fussery. That said, there's a reason it's there: for a shirt cuff to be properly ironed flat from the inside (see "Caring for Your Wardrobe"), the placket must be long enough to spread out the cuff. Also, a long placket makes rolling up your sleeves easier. And a placket that long might gape when being worn, so the button is there to prevent any potential gaping. About half of my shirts have this button and half don't. That said, I can't say I notice a lot of gaping or sleeve-rolling-trouble with the shorter placket shirts, so when I get a custom shirt, I forgo the extra button.

YOKES AND PLEATS

Although you'll almost never see them, there are also a number of features on a shirt's back to be aware of. At the top of the shirt, below the collar and above the shoulder blades, extends the yoke. Yokes may be either a single piece of fabric or two. When two, known as a "split yoke," they are often cut on the bias (with the two pieces of fabric at forty-five degrees to each other). When a custom-made shirt has a split yoke, it is done to compensate for any irregularities in a person's frame. In readywear, a split yoke is largely for show and not necessarily a sign of quality.

Pleats are sometimes added just below the yoke. If you prefer a looser fit, this is where the extra fabric in the back of the shirt may be gathered up. There are several types of pleats, with the most historical being many small gatherings along the entirety of the yoke. Nowadays, you are more likely to see a pleat in the centre on a casual shirt (called a box pleat, and sometimes inverted) or pleats near both shoulders on a dressier shirt. Since I strongly believe that for a shirt to be both comfortable and functional there must be ease built into the body, the extra fabric in my shirt backs necessitates pleats. I have all types of pleats depending on how formal or casual the shirt is. Also, since I like ease in the mid-section, I rarely have darts put into my shirts.

> The locker loop is a feature that used to be common on sporty shirts. A small strip of fabric at the centre/bottom of the yoke, usually above a box pleat, the loop is made for exactly the purpose the name suggests: hanging your shirt in a locker.

CUFFS

The last — but still important — feature on a shirt is a set of cuffs. There are almost as many cuff styles as shirt makers, but they can all be boiled down to a few basics. First off, you either

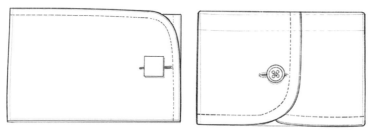

Rounded French (or double) cuff   Rounded barrel cuff

have a French cuff or a barrel, the former usually affixed with cufflinks, the latter with buttons. Almost all barrel cuffs are closed
with a single button; trying to do up or undo two or more buttons on a cuff is like a form of medieval torture. Another style is
the cocktail or Napoleon cuff, a barrel cuff that is turned back on
itself. While this is a supremely elegant style, it's as rare today as
spats. French cuffs can be single or double, and can be rounded,
angled, or squared, just like barrel. A single French cuff is the
most formal, with double cuffs a close second. Barrel cuffs are the
most casual, which explains why French cuffs on a button-down
shirt would look clownish.

Most of my shirts have single button, rounded-barrel cuffs.
Since French cuffs have an old-timey fanciness to them, I reserve
them for just a couple of my dressiest shirts.

Construction

You don't need to know how a shirt is made in order to find a good one. But looking for a few telltale signs of quality construction can help you determine if a shirt is worth investing in. First, though, I need to dispel a certain myth that has gained legitimacy on the internet: the legend of the handmade shirt. The legend holds that if a shirt is made completely by hand, with every stitch crafted by the hands of an artisan, it is automatically the finest shirt on the market. Nonsense.

In truth, it is nearly impossible to make a shirt completely by hand, and there is no evidence that this would actually produce a shirt that would be durable as well as attractive. Here is the honest truth when it comes to some hand finishing: it's unnecessary for the functionality of the shirt, like hand-rolled bottom edges. But these touches are not superfluous. In fact, some handmade details can speak to the overall quality of a shirt. Almost no one would bother cutting and finishing buttonholes by hand if they had not also invested work and care in the rest of the shirt.

That said, plenty of the world's best shirts are made fully by machine, or a combination of machine and hand stitching. They are simply two approaches to the same problem: making a shirt that is durable, attractive, and well fitting. For instance, one of the trickiest areas in shirt construction is the armhole, an area where there is a lot of movement, tension, and stress. A hand-attached sleeve attempts to deal with that by relying on the natural give of hand stitching. However, a machine-stitched sleeve head might actually be shaped differently, to compensate for the stiffness of machine stitching, but produce a similar result, just with different aesthetics. The question of overall quality doesn't come down to the type of construction used, machine or hand, but to the quality of that construction.

However, there are a few features you can look for that do mean quality. Stitching is the first: look for the smallest stitches possible. These are finer and more durable, and they require better machines to produce. Second is single-needle seams, sometimes called French seams. These you will find on the sides of the shirt: look for a thin, flat seam with only one line of stitches. In and of themselves, single-needle stitches do not symbolize quality: they can still be poorly applied. But when done well, they are not only more difficult to produce than double-needle stitches, they also produce a smoother, less bulky seam, one you are less likely to feel as you wear the shirt and one less likely to deteriorate over time. A third telltale sign of quality construction is pattern matching, like when the stripes on a shirt align perfectly with a pocket or across the front placket. It takes just that much more skill in the design and cutting of a shirt to match patterns across the front, pockets, plackets, yoke, and collar. Buttons are a fourth indicator of quality: a manufacturer is not likely to use real mother-of-pearl on an otherwise low-quality shirt. And finally, a tiny detail most people would barely notice are side gussets. Found at the bottom of the side seams, these little pieces of fabric are vestiges of when shirts tended to tear at the shoulders, armpits, and bottoms. Side gussets are not necessary anymore (there is typically very little strain on the bottom of a shirt), but their inclusion indicates a touch of extra care that could indicate quality elsewhere in the shirt.

Fit

How a shirt should fit is the hardest element to define. Preferred fit is completely dependent on your comfort, your concept of style, and your image of yourself. A shirt that may be perfect for one guy who likes a bit more ease and freedom will seem three sizes too big for the next guy. However, my criteria are centred on comfort, not fashion: if you cannot move in a shirt, no matter how great it looks, you will eventually hate wearing it (not to mention, it will tear at the elbows, side seams, and anywhere else there is a strain).

When you first put on a shirt, there are a number of ways to quickly and easily test the fit.

1. When you do up the collar, there should be room for two fingers, not much more, not much less.
2. When you do up the cuffs, they should rest on your hands but not slide over them.
3. When you bend your arms, there should be little to no pulling at the elbow, and your cuffs should stay in place (not move up your arm).

4. You should be able to bring your elbows together in front of you without too much strain on the back of the shirt.

5. When you sit down, there should be no strain on the buttons over your belly.

Another feature to look for is the placement of the shoulder seam. The top of the seam should sit on your shoulder bone, the one that sticks out just before your arm slopes downward. The area between your collar and your shoulder seam should be smooth, not buckling.

The sizes of shirt armholes are difficult to define as they depend on the maker and the style of shirt you prefer. For instance, higher (i.e., smaller) armholes on jackets produce a better range of motion but can have the opposite effect on a shirt.

Assessing Quality

Unlike many of the garments in this book, very little is hidden in a shirt. Other than the insides of collars and cuffs, the craftsmanship is fully on display. And that provides an excellent opportunity to assess quality. Do not be shy: before making a purchase, lay the shirt out and closely examine all the inside seams, looking for clean, small, even stitches.

Of course, that doesn't tell you everything. The final assessment comes down to you and the way you wear the shirt. Once it is on, look at the way the collar balances with the rest of the shirt. Look at the lines and curves. Do they look lyrical and elegant? Does the shirt look like a collection of elements — fabric, stitches, features — or do they harmonize into something greater than the shirt's parts? And finally, how does the shirt make you look? Like a better version of yourself? Then that's the shirt for you.

Sport Jackets

In our time, it is primarily sports clothes that have broken away from the previous traditions of male attire. They above all mark the democratic century, with its swing towards freedom and ease.

— The Duke of Windsor

The first time I saw a tailor working on a sport jacket, I couldn't believe what I was witnessing. The tailor began taking it apart in front of my eyes, and what until that point had looked like a regular jacket revealed its inner life. Between the outer cloth, at that point covered in long white stitches, and the inner, shiny lining was layer upon layer of fabric. As the tailor separated the layers to rework them after a fitting, I saw that some of them were dense and, literally, hairy. Some of it looked like a layer of sponge, covered in stitch marks. Other pieces of spongy stuff sat at the shoulder. Even bits of dark fabric were glued around all the seams and insides of pockets. I asked the tailor what all this was for and he looked at me like I was an idiot. "To give it shape," he said plainly. And that is the key to finding a quality jacket. But before I dig into that, some history.

Sport jackets and blazers each have their own origins and evolution, eventually becoming almost the same garment. A boldly striped jacket or a blue jacket with gold buttons is a blazer by historical association. Meanwhile, all other types of sport jackets bear little resemblance to their antecedent, the Norfolk jacket. With many pockets, a belt, and deep pleats behind the shoulders, the Norfolk was built for riding and shooting. While it doesn't look much like today's sport jackets, it was primarily worn with non-matching trousers, which perhaps, over time, got us accustomed to jackets and trousers of different colours or patterns. Also, strip the Norfolk of its sporty accoutrements and it is simply a sport jacket.

However, sport jackets and blazers today have more in common with suit jackets of the nineteenth century. In fact, the first lounge suit jackets, as they were called, share most if not all the same features. Originally called "sack" jackets — the name originating perhaps in France for the way they were constructed, not the way they looked — were a casual alternative to the frock coat. Instead of being made of a number of panels like a frock, the *sacque* was made like a sack, with four segments stitched together. These jackets were also lighter in construction than their forebears. But that is relative. The first jackets had much more internal structure than jackets do today, to give them even more of a defined shape, and the fabrics themselves were many times heavier. In fact, jacket linings were heavier than many jacket fabrics (called "suiting") today.

But as much as we tend to think of jackets as formal, I think it's important to remember their sporty and casual history if only to inspire us to wear jackets in a more casual way. And this is the great benefit of owning a dark-blue jacket: you can wear it dressed up or dressed down; with a tie and grey flannel trousers; or with an open collar shirt and chinos. Some wear sport jackets with jeans, although that's not my style.

Now, you'll hear a number of ways that jackets are referred to: sport jacket (usually "sports" jacket in the U.S.), sport coat, and blazer. They are all, fundamentally, the same garment. "Jacket" or "coat" goes back to what different tailors in different parts of the world called them — still today a jacket is almost always a "coat" on Savile Row. As I mentioned, these jackets have a sporting history, and the blazer is no different. However, I'm not going to wade into the anthropological argument about the history of the name. Whether it was a boat or a rowing club, it doesn't really matter. Most likely the context was nautical, and the garment was considered somewhat formal. Thus, the dark-blue fabric and brass buttons. I don't get too caught up in these names. I have a dark-blue jacket, which I sometimes call a blazer, but instead of brass buttons, it has dark-brown horn buttons. I prefer the more understated look.

The great danger to wearing a dark-blue jacket is that it will look like an orphaned suit jacket. You may notice that many sport jackets are made in fabrics and patterns you'd never see in a suit. That is partially to differentiate them from suits. The same with buttons. Colours may contrast with the jacket or the buttons may be covered in leather. While I don't prefer a lot of contrast, some variation is important, again, to make sure you don't look like you just grabbed the jacket from your suit.

Contrast is the key, however, for how to wear a jacket: contrast with your trousers. The colours don't have to be opposite, but if they are too similar, you will look like you are wearing a cheap suit. Dark and light is always a good starting point, such as a dark-blue jacket and light-grey trousers.

Orphaned Jackets

The reason not to wear your typical worsted wool suit jacket as a separate is that it looks out of place, "orphaned" as those in the industry say. It's likely the buttons are tone-on-tone with the jacket, and perhaps there's even a subtle pattern or stripe. Though most people don't wear tailored clothes anymore, they can still spot this sartorial abnormality. And somewhere in the subconscious, we know it doesn't look quite right.

Lapels

A jacket should never be boring, prim, or rigid. It should be sexy. I'm not talking about the fabric or the colour or even the fit. I'm talking about the lapels. On a well-crafted jacket, the lapels roll and rise off the front of the jacket like a living thing. Like the petals of a flower.

Lapels proclaim that, yes, masculinity does include things some people call feminine. And it has for generations, long before our so-called progressive age. And male sexuality should include these things. It is so much more than the macho image of today. It can also be curvy and sensual, while also powerful. Like the first step of a tango.

NOTCH, PEAK, AND SHAWL

There are three types of jacket lapels: notch, peak, and shawl. Shawl is best left to formal wear because it is so unique and unusual, with its long, uninterrupted line. Peak is also usually in the realm of tuxedos but not historically so. Jackets, even more casual jackets, have had peak lapels for over a century. However, peak lapels give the jacket a more aggressive look, pointing upward, so I prefer to reserve them for the one style of jacket made for a peak lapel: the double-breasted (discussed in the next section). For most sport jackets, I prefer the workhorse of lapels: the notch. It is simple and unassuming and yet, with the right proportions and shape, can be quietly elegant and lyrical.

Be mindful of where the notch in your lapel is located: too high up, resting on your shoulders, and the lapels are disproportionately long. Too low, down on your breast, and a jacket can look saggy and slouchy.

Regardless of the style of your lapel, look for some shape, even a subtle curve. This gives the jacket an overall better appearance: straight lines are boring. There should also be a "roll" to the lapel, which means there shouldn't be a firm fold of fabric where it meets the buttoning part of the jacket. Instead, the lapel should roll away from the rest of the jacket. Again, giving an overall appearance of living sensuality.

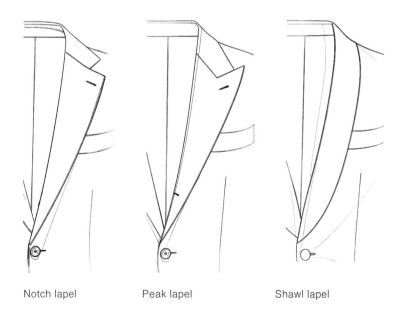

Notch lapel   Peak lapel   Shawl lapel

Single- and Double-Breasted

The most common and easy to wear jacket is single-breasted. Buttoned or unbuttoned, it does its job exceptionally well, adding refinement and elegance to a shirt and trousers. However, I like having one double-breasted sport jacket on hand for a dash of flair. A DB jacket should not be unbuttoned, even when you sit down, because it can lose its silhouette. And the silhouette is what I love most about a DB, especially in a more casual sport jacket fabric. It is at once casual — soft and textured like a cozy sweater — and formal, due to the shape of the lapels.

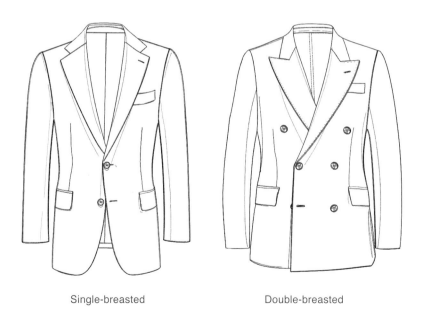

Single-breasted   Double-breasted

Shoulders

One of the most defining elements of a jacket are its shoulders. They can hug the body, providing a casual silhouette. At the other extreme, they can sit high and wide from the body, making the wearer look taller or broader. A bit of roping, where the sleeve rises above the shoulder, giving it an almost pagoda-like look, is the boldest example. Obviously, in today's more casual world, the former is quite popular. But shoulder shape should be defined by your body, the style of jacket, and how you will wear it. An Italian tailor once told me that he was offended when he saw business jackets — dark colours, worsted wool, worn in the office — with soft shoulders. In his eyes, that is a sartorial contradiction. He wouldn't suggest a large, built-up shoulder (he is Italian, after all) but would advise some shape and structure to add a touch of formality. Not to mention the fabric: some fabrics, due to their lightness, require more external materials to provide shape. Otherwise, the jacket can appear lifeless. That said, heavier fabrics can sometimes stand on their own and give enough shape without needing internal structure (I'm looking at you, corduroy).

You should also consider your body type. Someone with broad, strong shoulders should probably avoid padding, except of the lightest kind. On the other hand, someone with sloped shoulders might appreciate some height. But again, this comes down to your own sense of personal style. If you feel most comfortable in a shaped, extended shoulder, then that is what you should wear regardless of your body type. However, I would

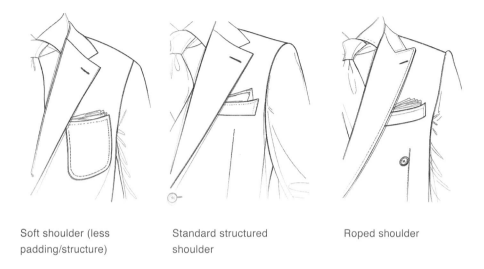

Soft shoulder (less
padding/structure)

Standard structured
shoulder

Roped shoulder

recommend trying as many different shoulder shapes as you can and even having a few options in your wardrobe, depending on the fabric of your jackets and how you intend to wear them, formally or casually.

Pockets

You will find one of three basic types of pockets on most jackets: jetted (also called "besom"), patch, and flapped (and sometimes flapped patch). Jetted are the most formal, looking like a simple slit through the fabric. Personally, I find jetted pockets too formal

Remove Those Stitches

Jetted pockets often arrived sewn shut on off-the-rack models, along with the breast pocket and sometimes the buttonholes. This is for show only, so that the jacket retains its shape during shipping and display. Remove the stitching (which is only lightly sewn in, anyway) as soon as you get the jacket home. This goes for the back vents, as well. I sometimes wish I carried scissors at all times so I could liberate jacket vents on the uninitiated.

for sport jackets. They almost always have a flap tucked in the pocket, which I recommend pulling out to add some visual interest to the bottom of the jacket.

My favourite style of pocket for a sport jacket or blazer, however, is the patch pocket. A favourite, too, of southern Italian tailors, the patch is the most casual pocket because it sits on top of the jacket. It invites you to put your hands in your pockets, another way to take formality down a few notches. Or to just throw some stuff into them: they are pockets, after all.

You will occasionally see a small pocket above the right pocket, called the "ticket" pocket. The assumption is that this is where

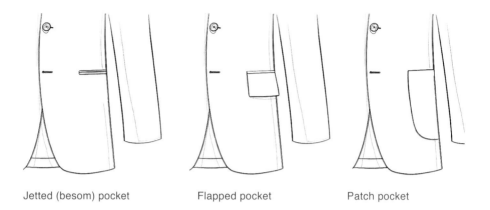

Jetted (besom) pocket   Flapped pocket   Patch pocket

you would have kept a train or event ticket, despite the average jacket having many, many other pocket options. Ticket pockets are certainly an opportunity for personality, but they add more visual complication and bulk to the mid-section, so use them sparingly.

Rarer still is the "hacking," or slanted, pocket. These pockets owe their shape to horseback riding: when leaning forward on a horse, the pockets would then be parallel to the ground, thus easier to access. I have not, though, ever attempted this feat,

If your jacket pattern is a bit bold, or if you have some weight around the middle, you can minimize the effect by tucking pocket flaps into the pockets, turning them back into jetted pockets. This removes a bit of visual distraction at the waist and hip area.

so I cannot attest to a hacking pocket's usefulness. Like ticket pockets, hacking pockets are a bold statement but can work on a jacket with peak lapels, creating a sort of X across the front of your jacket. If you want to wear a giant X, that is.

Vents

The more I wear jackets, the more I am convinced that the number of vents, when it comes to practicality, makes absolutely no difference. I've heard some people say that double vents are useful for someone with a "full seat" because instead of protruding, your backside is hidden behind the flap. Someone who is wider at the hips should therefore consider a single vent, to keep the jacket from splaying outward. But having lived my adult life with a full seat and having worn jackets with one, two, and no vents, I don't see that any of these arguments hold much water.

Vents were first added to sport jackets for horseback riding. With the jacket buttoned up while riding, the vent was the only way to keep the jacket from bunching up on the waist. But since most of us unbutton our jackets before sitting down, the issue is moot. Instead, vents come down to fashion and personal taste. Fashion will dictate what type of vent is available on most off-the-rack jackets. For the past couple of decades, the double vent has been most popular. My biggest concern with double vents is that if the jacket is not well cut (too tight in the skirt, causing the vents to pull away from the jacket), it looks like you have a big ol' mud flap covering your butt.

I have a mix of single and double vents, but a good friend is always encouraging me to forgo vents altogether. Maybe I will on my next jacket.

Buttons

Practically speaking, a sport jacket really needs only one button on the front. Placed right about at your waist (the thinnest part of your torso), it's all that's needed to hold your jacket closed. Since most jackets today have open quarters — the bottom parts of the fronts of jackets, that sweep away from each other instead of over-lapping — the bottom button on almost all jackets is vestigial. It is not meant to be used because the jacket is constructed in such a way that doing it up would cause the jacket skirt to buckle and lose its shape. On a three-button jacket, if you do up both the middle and top buttons, you end up with less lapel and therefore less ex-posed shirt front. Whether you have a two- or three-button jacket is a question of personal style.

As to the number of buttons on your jacket cuffs, that's pure-ly a matter of personal preference. The convention has been that fewer buttons are more casual, but then again I have seen older vintage tuxedos with only one or two buttons. I go down the middle, with three buttons on all my jackets. And I prefer to

3-Roll-2 Jackets

When it comes to jacket buttoning, I prefer the "3-roll-2" set-up. As the story goes, when two-button jackets became popular in the 1930s, students too poor or too frugal to replace all their three-button jackets simply pressed their lapels to the second button, thus rolling the lapel over the top button. This exposed the rough, unfinished underside of the top buttonhole, but beggars can't be choosers. This became known as "3-roll-2" or a three-button jacket rolled to the second button. And before long, makers like Brooks Brothers started creating jackets with this feature built in: essentially two-button jackets with a third button hidden in the roll of the lapel, while the visible buttonhole was now finished on the opposite, showing side.

space the buttons out from each other, instead of having "kissing" buttons, which can either touch or overlap. I once saw a photo of Rudolph Valentino with three spaced buttons on the cuff of his jacket and damn if that, and his smouldering look, didn't win me over.

Working cuff buttons are a complicated issue. In historical terms, working buttons were referred to as "doctor's cuffs" because they could be undone and rolled up in an emergency. I have heard that high-end tailoring customers were actually first to request non-working cuff buttons to show that they, themselves, were non–working class. But as ready-to-wear clothing spread in the middle of the twentieth century, non-working buttons were a necessity (allowing for sleeve length alterations). So the world of tailoring reclaimed working cuff buttons as a symbol of bespoke craftsmanship. Recently, some men have even left some buttons undone to prove that their cuffs are indeed working. I played with this at first but soon got over it. Buttons are for buttoning.

But you know what? Working or not, it doesn't matter what kind of buttons you have on your cuffs. You're not going to roll up your sleeves, so don't fret. A custom jacket will almost always have working buttons because, why not? The jacket was made just for you, and you're not going to alter it. But there is no shame in wearing non-working buttons.

Construction

Years ago, I was in the studio of a custom tailor. He had immigrated, decades before, to Canada from Italy. At that time, he did practically everything by hand. But after years of working in industrial production, all his jackets were fused. "Fused" means that part of the internal structure in the chest is glued to the jacket fabric instead of meticulously attached by hand. He assured me that fusing was better: it was faster and cheaper and worked just as well. My heart broke.

The truth, I've discovered, is that fused does not compare to fully canvassed, where the interlining structure, canvas, is stitched to the outer fabric. Stitched canvas is more substantial than fused interlining. This internal structure doesn't just firm up the front of the jacket, but also gives it shape: the rounded shape it needs to lie properly over the chest. Fusing gives some shape but not enough, for instance, to create that full, sensual lapel roll mentioned previously. Instead, fused lapels tend to lie flat against the chest. A fused jacket is also not as durable because the glue can eventually dislodge, and the jacket will not retain its shape over many years. A fully canvassed jacket, on the other hand, will keep its shape for the life of the garment. Canvas is very robust, traditionally made of horsehair and other fabrics, and it is curled and manipulated when it is attached in order to give the chest shape.

However, a full canvas is expensive because, either done by hand or by machine, it involves more time and skill. A less costly alternative is "half-canvassed." This is where the top half or two thirds of the canvas is stitched in, but the bottom half, which plays a lesser role in jacket shape, is fused, if interlined at all. Half-canvas is a good compromise when trying to balance shape and durability with cost.

Quality, when it comes to the internal structure of a jacket, is a question of degrees. As with other garments, quality comes from a number of elements and how they work together. If each element is made and put together well, that is where the quality comes from and not necessarily from hand versus machine.

Matching Stripes

Once, while I was working in a tailoring shop, a customer ordered a striped suit and demanded that the stripes line up across the shoulders, from front to back. This is a nearly impossible feat because the fabric on either side of the shoulder is cut at different angles. With a colossal amount of effort — and swearing — the tailor was able to do it, slowly and carefully pulling and stretching the fabric into place. My feeling is that a few of the stripes should match on the shoulder, but to match all of them is a sign of sartorial derangement.

Speaking of which, do not get too caught up in all the talk around "handmade." A certain amount of handwork is ideal because the hand can give a type of shape to a stitch that a machine cannot, like around the collar and sleeve heads. However, certain stitches that don't need that kind of attention, especially the long seams down the arms and back, can and should be done by machine.

As a customer, assessing construction is one of your biggest challenges. You can't open up a jacket in a shop, and even if you could, unless you are a tailor, it would be tough to assess what you found inside. There are also tricks used to convince you of handwork. For instance, one kind of machine can produce a pick stitch (the mostly ornamental stitch that runs along the edge of the lapels) so realistic, it can fool almost anyone. In general, I find, things like pick stitching or contrast buttonholes are used to distract you for poor-quality overall construction and to set a brand apart in a crowded retail environment.

One sign of quality I look for in construction of jackets is the same as for shirts: pattern matching. If the jacket fabric has a strong stripe or check, look closely at the breast, flap, or patch pockets, and where the collar meets the back of the jacket. The patterns should flow as if they are the same piece of fabric. This is challenging, requiring a lot of skill in the cutting and planning stages of construction. (Don't worry too much across the chest: it is impossible to pattern match around darts that are there to give the jacket shape). However, pattern matching alone is not a guarantee of quality, it's just a step along the right direction.

Fit

It is too easy to be swayed by "comfort" when it comes to trying on a jacket. Most off-the-rack jackets are made to fit as many body types as possible, so too much room is put into the inside. This sometimes produces a shapeless jacket. Instead of comfort, look for ease of motion and how the jacket reacts to movement. Avoid the temptation to stand stock still in front of the mirror while you decide if a jacket fits you. Walk around, sit down, move.

There should be no gap between your neck and the collar of the jacket, at the back or around the sides. The collar should remain resting on your neck even if you raise your arms. The sleeve heads and shoulders should allow enough space that you can comfortably cross your arms in front of you without straining the jacket or constricting your movement. A higher (smaller) armhole is key for this. It is essential that the jacket fit well in the shoulders: not only are they the foundation to how a jacket is made, but also almost everything else can be adjusted by a tailor.

When the main front button is done up, the jacket should lie flat across your belly or have just the slightest tension when you walk around. However, this varies dramatically depending on the tailor, the style, and your personal preference. In my experience, North American tailors prefer a looser fit in the body, and even with the front button done up, you could still fit a chunky sweater underneath. Neapolitan tailors, at the other extreme, prefer the buttoning point so tight that swallowing one more mouthful of pasta will snap the button right off.

Jacket length really depends on your body proportions. The jacket should be long enough to reach the bottom of your seat, but if you have longer legs, you need a longer jacket to achieve visual balance. A longer torso, on the other hand, requires a shorter jacket. The old standby — that a jacket should end about halfway between the nape of your neck and the floor — still holds, but it's a guideline, not a rule.

A problem I find with off-the-rack jackets is that in an attempt to create a smooth chest, companies make them too tight. As soon as you do up the button or put a pocket square in the breast pocket, the lapel bends or "breaks." However, this can also be due to a sizing issue: just because you have a forty-inch chest doesn't mean that every size 40 jacket will fit you the same way. Shape, silhouette, and cut can vary immensely from maker to maker. Try different options even if they aren't technically your size.

> Any off-the-rack jacket will need and be improved by alterations. Sleeve length and waist adjustment in/out are the most effective. Adjusting shoulders is almost impossible.

Fabrics

The biggest way a sport jacket differs from a suit jacket is in the fabric it's crafted of — the "suiting," sometimes called "jacketing."

A sport jacket tends to be bolder in some way, either in colour, pattern, or texture. For instance, I wouldn't wear a full herringbone tweed suit for fear of it being too loud. But a herringbone tweed jacket worn with grey flannel trousers? My winter uniform.

As such, sport jackets can be made in any fabric composition or style you would use for a suit, be it wool, cotton, corduroy, linen, silk, cashmere, or vicuna.

Assessing Overall Quality

(For assessing quality in suiting, see pages 109–10.)

A jacket is not a flat piece of clothing, like trousers. A jacket should have shape and form even before you put it on. On a hanger, it should look three-dimensional, like someone is already wearing it. Even lying on your bed, it should lift up from the mattress, the shoulders round, the lapels flowering into the room.

The only part of a quality jacket that is flat is the collar, which should hug the neck. Shoulders should be hollow and round, the sleeves should pitch forward like your arms, the lapels should travel outward then slope back into the jacket, and the chest should have enough fabric in it that when not being worn, it drapes slightly, suggesting the volume within.

Trousers

*There are moments, Jeeves, when one
asks oneself, "Do trousers matter?"
"The mood will pass, sir."*

— P.G. Wodehouse, *The Code of the Woosters*

Trousers are a feat of architectural engineering. You may look at them and only see two tubes of fabric meeting at the top. And while there is a lot going on in the waistband and especially at the "fork" (where the bottom of the zipper meets the two legs), it is the legs themselves that have an almost impossible task. They must look streamlined and nicely shaped when standing (okay, easy enough), when walking (a bit trickier), and when sitting (how in God's name?). Consider this: when you are seated, the front of your legs have expanded into considerably more area than the back of your legs. Unless you are wearing stretch fabric (which I try to avoid because it is made of petroleum), your trousers must be engineered in such a way as to accommodate all this fluctuation in shape and area.

Of course, most trousers don't accomplish this feat of engineering. But as is often the case, the problem is the garment, not you. Last year I wanted a new pair of summer trousers — casually styled, lightweight fabric — so I ventured to a large menswear retailer. I tried my best to find the pairs that had quality fabric and construction, but it all went sideways in the fitting room. Every pair was a disaster. If they fit slim in the leg, they were so tight in the waist that I couldn't do them up. If they did fit in the waist, they were baggy and shapeless. Some would bulge at the knee when I was standing. Or they would pull at the tops of my thighs when I sat. I left them all in the change room and walked out of the store. I ended up re-ordering a pair I already owned that had faded and frayed from use (they're now my gardening trousers).

That day, I didn't even bother with a more in-depth way to judge a pair of trousers: move in them. Stand, absolutely, but also walk, sit, climb stairs. The trousers should work with you, not against you. Of course, beyond these initial impressions of fit and shape, there's a lot to consider when looking for trousers.

In this section I'm talking about almost anything you put on your legs other than jeans. Okay, and except sweatpants. They don't even deserve three sentences.

Jeans

This chapter is not about jeans. There are enough jeans in the world, by far, and the last thing I need to do is convince more people to buy more jeans. What I will say on the matter, however, is that if you are interested in jeans, do yourself and the planet a favour and buy untreated denim from a quality maker. No distressing, no pre-washing, no sweatshops. Fast fashion jeans are terrible for the environment and garment workers. Instead, spend the money on quality construction and do the aging yourself: live in your jeans, wash them occasionally (in cold water, inside out, hang-dry), and let them age with you. And even though it's hard, do your best to find out who made them and under what conditions. Jeans, sadly, have become the fast food of the clothing world.

Rise

Trouser rise is the distance between where the legs meet, at the bottom of the crotch, and the top of the waistband. I categorize it this way: eight inches is a low rise, ten inches is a medium rise, and anything above eleven inches is a high rise. None of my trousers

Full-rise trousers

are below ten inches and many are eleven. And why does rise matter so much that I'm starting the "Trousers" section with it?

A younger friend once asked me for some suit-shopping advice. I accompanied him to a vintage clothing shop and helped him find an excellent two-piece tweed suit. On the peg it looked his size, but when he tried it on the trousers hung down really low in the crotch and bunched up at the ankles. He stood there looking dishevelled and confused.

"They're supposed to sit at your natural waist," I told him. "You have to hike them up." When he lifted the waistband to its proper position, he was transformed: the trousers hung cleanly off his waist, elongating his legs, and the cuffs sat perfectly on his shoes. "This feels weird," he told me, "all this fabric around my belly." At that moment I realized that this guy had lived his entire thirty-plus years wearing only low-rise trousers.

Before you accuse me of longing for the age of monocles and top hats, natural-waisted trousers (also called "high-waisted") are not an affectation of the past that have had their day. Trousers that sit at the natural waist are just that: natural. If they are tailored correctly, they are most flattering for most men. They also work best with tailored jackets, so that when the jacket is buttoned, you don't get that unfortunate triangle of shirt sticking out the bottom. That triangle only serves to distract from where people are supposed to be looking: your face.

Natural-waisted trousers did not pass from favour because they didn't work. Instead, they were swept out to sea by the tsunami that is jeans (even when I try not to include them, they find their way into this chapter again). Traditionally cut low and sitting at the hips, by the 1980s jeans became the model for more and more trouser cuts. Eventually, low-rise became so ubiquitous my friend grew up never wearing trousers that fit as they should. And as he ages, chances are he will look worse and worse if all his trousers are low-rise.

The jean cut looks best on young, slim figures. (Then again, so do natural-waisted trousers). As your figure matures and if weight starts to appear in the middle, low-cut trousers only push this bulge out. Natural-waisted trousers help to smooth the transition from the torso over the belly and to the legs. As a sartorially minded friend often says "your abdomen should be in your trousers, not in your shirt."

This issue has reached absurd proportions, literally, in combination with the other obsession of our age: short jackets. What happens is this: a short jacket makes your torso look shorter, with the buttoning point often above the waist (even if it's only a quarter inch, it looks high). Combined with low-rise trousers, you are cut into three: torso, belly, and legs. With well-fitting jackets and natural-rise trousers, you have only two zones, torso and legs, which leaves you looking well proportioned.

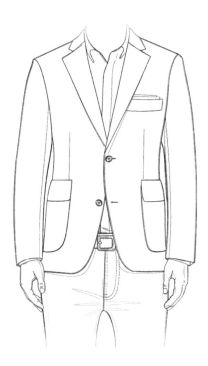

Unflattering proportions: high-buttoning short jacket with low-rise trousers

I'm not saying that all trousers on all guys should sit at the natural waist, but neither should all trousers sit at the hips. We should let our body shapes and natural proportions guide our style choices, not fashion and trends.

Pleats

Body shapes and natural proportions are also my basis for pleats. They should be thought of as neither fashionable nor unfashionable. Pleats are functional. And you either enjoy that function or you don't. Liking or disliking the look should come second.

Pleats were, as far as I can find, an invention of post–First World War tailors: a clever way to introduce volume to the part of the trouser that needs it, to accommodate the way the abdomen expands when you sit. Not to mention a help for sticking your hands in your pockets without stressing the side seams. Well-made pleats mean comfort in your midsection, thanks to the extra fabric, while maintaining a slim silhouette by tucking that extra fabric into the pleats. In fact, pleats should close and sit so smooth across the front that they almost have the same silhouette as flat-front trousers.

But yes, I know, you're picturing those huge, ballooning pleated chinos from the 90s. That was simply the case of certain brands, in a misdirected attempt for "comfort," introducing too much fabric into the front of trousers. Yes, the more pleats the more volume, but pleats don't need to be super deep, and again, they should be based on need and style. Personally, I find two pleats is the most fabric I need, and I can usually manage with one.

The direction of the pleats is purely personal preference. Outward facing, with softer fabric, can produce a lovely sweeping look. Heavier fabric, however, can result in what looks like a flap on the front of your trousers. I prefer inward facing pleats; although, they can produce a lot of shadow and, thus, visual attention at your crotch, where you don't want people looking. Unless, of course, you do.

I also feel that the higher the rise, the more essential pleats are. As the rise rises, more and more of your abdomen is contained in your trousers, which means you need more fabric. My pair of high-rise flat-front chinos suffer from sticky-outy pockets for this reason.

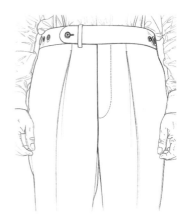

Single, inward-facing pleats

Double, outward-facing pleats

Cuffs

Like so many other aspects of classic menswear, people believe the exact opposite about cuffs than what is true: that they are more formal than cuffless trousers. I can only assume this is because the fashion for cuffs on suits was so prevalent in the 80s and 90s that the association stuck. The truth is quite the opposite. In the late nineteenth century it was common in Britain, when doing outdoor activities, to turn up the bottoms of your trousers to protect them from water or mud. It became formalized, and fashionable, around the turn of the last century, thanks to King Edward VII. He had cuffs "tailored-in" to his country trousers, making them permanent. When his grandson came along, the eventual Duke of Windsor wore cuffed trousers regularly, entrenching them in men's fashion. The outdoorsy association is why, by the way, you will never, or should never, find cuffs on a tuxedo or white tie ensemble.

Now that we've sorted that out, should you have cuffs on your trousers? Again, I return to the issue of functionality, but not really the "traipsing around a boggy moor" functionality. A useful function of cuffs is to add weight to the bottom of trousers, allowing them to hang better. This is especially useful with lighter-weight fabrics. Although, truth be told, the trousers would probably hang just about as well without cuffs. Unless, of course, you filled the cuffs with pennies. The other function of cuffs is to create a visual break between your trousers and your shoes. I have cuffs on almost all my trousers for that reason: the visual impact. It's like a period at the end of a sentence.

I'm not one for fixed rules, but when it comes to cuff height, it is useful to consider this one: the longer the leg, the higher the cuff. It's all about proportions. I am six foot two inches and prefer my cuffs at 1.75 inches. I found 1.5 inches too slim and 2 inches too bulky.

Belts and Suspenders

No, never wear them at the same time. However, you don't have to pick sides either. Both are functional and useful in their own ways.

I prefer suspenders on mid- to high-rise trousers, in colder months. In particular, that's because having a belt cut into my abdomen on that rise doesn't feel good and can make you look like a muffin. In colder months, when I wear sweaters and jackets, I wear suspenders because they are more comfortable and I don't like to show them off.

My other reason for wearing suspenders is comfort. A loose waist is more physically comfortable than a constrained waist. That said, when it's warmer and I'm not covering my shirt — and therefore my suspenders — and my trousers are lower rise, then I wear a belt.

I'm a big fan of woven, elasticized belts for the extra comfort and the more casual look they provide than a standard leather belt. Woven leather is a nice compromise between the two.

Why I Hide My Suspenders

Suspenders were originally considered underwear. But that's not why I avoid showing my suspenders. Instead, I blame Mork from Ork. When I grew up in the 70s, there was a show called *Mork and Mindy* starring a young and hyper-energized Robin Williams. He played an alien who wore bright, striped clothing, including rainbow suspenders. They become a fashion staple of the 70s. Then in the 80s, thanks to films like *Wall Street*, suspenders were once again a fashion accessory. They haven't really recovered. I avoid any suggestion of hearkening back to that look by keeping my suspenders out of sight.

Fabric

I separate my trousers, like the rest of my wardrobe, into two seasons: warm and cold weather. The fabrics my trousers are made of follow those seasonal needs.

WARM-WEATHER FABRICS

When I was eighteen, I spent the summer living with my cousins in Portugal. They were a few years older than me and showed me around

Lisbon, taking me to cafés, bars, and concerts. I had a fantastic time. But every time we met up outside my grandmother's apartment, I would catch them exchanging a smile or a chuckle. After a few days, I confronted them and demanded they tell me what was so funny.

"Your shorts," one of them said. "Only kids wear shorts."

I didn't so much feel shame as I felt a sense of passage, from childhood to adulthood. Here was a culture that held on to this old coming-of-age tradition. And I have never worn shorts in a city environment since then. But in truth, shorts don't necessarily connote youth to me as much as they suggest relaxation or even sport. So I keep them for backyard barbecues and the beach. But I'd never wear them to a movie, to work, or out for dinner. And if you're thinking that trousers are too hot, consider the people who have, for millennia, lived in the hottest places on earth. They discovered long ago that long garments, made of lightweight fabrics and weaves for breathability, are actually more comfortable because they protect you from the heat of the sun.

And nothing beats linen in the summer. The fabric is naturally light enough to keep you covered without warming up. And I find the wrinkles to be stylish in a devil-may-care way. However, pure linen trousers can be a bit too flouncy when worn with anything except beach wear. I prefer a cotton/linen blend for a combination of lightness with the shape and structure of cotton. Straight-up cotton is also a great summer option, especially lightweight chinos. Lightness also applies to colour in the summer. I have only one pair of summer trousers in a dark colour (blue, for versatility), preferring cream, grey-green, tan, and light brown.

Despite its associations with winter months, wool is another excellent choice of fabric in summer. Some wools are woven of such thin threads, into such open weaves, that they wear as light as linen without creasing.

COLD-WEATHER FABRICS

Wool is the ideal fabric when the weather starts to cool down. My favourite option is flannel. Ranging from light to heavy, flannel is at once sharp and casual: sharp, because it hangs so nicely and smoothly; casual because of its fuzzy, nappy texture.

Cotton is another great cool-weather choice, in either heavier twill-woven chinos or corduroy. Corduroy, or "the workingman's velvet" as I call it, gives your trousers visual interest without having to introduce more colour and pattern, which can overwhelm the rest of your outfit. Corduroy comes in a variety of weights, and even the width of the wale (the three-dimensional stripes on the corduroy weave) can make trousers look either relaxed (wide wale) or sharp (thin wale).

Cool-weather colours for me are mid- to dark browns and greys, as well as the occasional dark green. These colours go with almost any top in almost any colour.

Fit

Many aspects of the fit of trousers, like other garments, are subjective. But I reference a few points for myself when trying them on for the first time. The main one is smooth lines. The fabric should flow relatively smoothly around your seat, front, and legs, neither bulging nor breaking. For instance, if the hip pockets are flaring, there is not enough fabric around the front. If your legs are constricted when you sit down, the trousers are too tight in the thighs. If your trousers bunch up on top of your shoes, they are too long. And while certain measurements are worth knowing — how wide you like trousers at the knee and the cuffs — these aren't universal. In my own closet I have a range from slim to loose.

The issue of trouser length is also highly personal and hard to get exactly right. I prefer my trousers to break just slightly on my shoes (which means a small amount of buckle) but this really can depend on the style and the cuff opening. Trousers with a tighter cuff, which stays closer to the leg, need to be shorter because they will bunch up more on your shoes. Wider trousers can be longer but can also feel like bell-bottoms if too long. I try not to obsess because depending on how much your trousers travel up and down on your waist

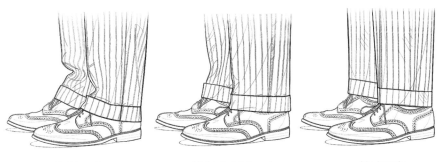

Full break   Mid (slight) break   No break

during the day — inevitable with a belt, slightly more controlled with suspenders — you'll never maintain the same length. I just try to keep all my trousers roughly in this range: long enough to cover my socks, but not long enough to cover my shoes.

Assessing Quality

As with shirts, a fair amount of the inner workings of trousers can be seen and examined, and there are a few signifiers of quality to look out for. Again, don't be shy about having a good look under the hood when shopping for trousers; it might even earn you a bit of respect from the salesperson.

I look first at the waistband, especially around the back. There's a lot going on in a waistband, but the better makers manage to get it all in to a relatively thin package. A bulky waistband is a sign that corners were cut in production or lower-quality assembly was used.

When it comes to the quality of assembly, like with other garments, don't be fooled by hand finishing. While, usually, no one would bother to hand tack pleats and pockets on a poor-quality trouser, these can be added as non-functioning embellishments, meant to distract you from poor-quality construction. It is more important that finishing and reinforcing stress points be well done, regardless if they are sewn by hand or machine.

Other construction features to look for include pocket stays: they are bits of fabric that connect the pockets to the fly. They keep the pockets from being pulled outward and out of shape. The pocket material itself can also be a clue: it should be substantial cotton, not flimsy T-shirt quality, which will wear through faster. And look closely at the finishing of all the seams on the inside of the trousers. The more even, clean, and consistent, the better.

Fabric plays a major role in the overall quality of trousers, of course. But until you've spent a lot of time experiencing different qualities of fabric, it can be hard to tell the good from the very good. However, there are a few telltale signs I look for to separate the good from the bad. Thinness and softness are not among them: plenty of great fabrics out there are heavy and scratchy. Instead, you have to assess the weave and construction. I look for some kind of life in the fabric. For instance, do I like the way it looks? And I don't mean the colour or the pattern. Look at the overall impression the fabric gives: Is there a depth to whatever colour it has? Does it have a shimmer or shine? (Stay away from shine.) I also look for cloth that feels alive. Does it have some body to it, or does it just lie flat? Does it bounce back into shape after you scrunch it up? Of course, this can all depend on whether you're looking at linen, wool, or cotton, but what's most important is that you look beyond the colour and pattern and take a good close look at, and feel, the fabric itself. Touch enough fabric and you will develop, over time, a sixth sense for quality.

Two-Piece Suits

From London the suit spread ... around the world until it became the international standard for correct male attire. But lest you think that this makes it drab or square, remember that the foremost avatars of cool in the last century, the great jazz musicians, wore it routinely.
— Nicholas Antongiavanni, *The Suit*

I was going to wear my first suit on a hot June day just before I turned seven. And my entire family — two dozen aunts, uncles, cousins, and other relations I'd never met — was going to witness it. I was to receive the sacrament of the Holy Eucharist, and a suit was a necessity. But a seven-year-old doesn't care about all that stuff. He cares about playing and having fun and wearing whatever he wants. I know. I have a son.

My parents bought the suit at a Catholic ceremonial-wear shop. The store is still there, just a few minutes away from where I now live. They sell baptism gowns, religious jewellery, and fancy linens. And Communion suits, like the one I wore: a cream polyester three-piece with a button-up shirt and oversized bow tie. Classic 1970s fashion with bell-bottom pants and lapels as big as wings. Looking back, I can admit that I kind of like the slanted pockets. Mercifully, because it was summer, my mother didn't make me wear the vest.

I didn't ever dress up as a kid, so getting into that suit on a humid day was not fun. The shirt was stiff and felt tight on my neck. And while the jacket was constricting, the bow tie made me feel fancy. Once at my Communion, packed into St. Agnes Church with hundreds of other boys in cheap suits and girls dressed as brides, I started to seriously overheat. Polyester famously doesn't breathe, and I sweat on a cold day if there's a warm breeze. My mother remembers fearing for my safety as she looked at my hair, wet from sweat, plastered to my forehead, my eyes vacant. The priest had insisted that parents stay away from their children during the ceremony, so she stood at the back of the church, nervously watching me. She seemed miles away.

I felt feverish and confused as I waited to be called. The priest's voice echoed around the huge church, and I didn't understand a word of his liturgical Portuguese. When it was finally my time, I was paired with a little girl and we walked up the aisle towards the altar, like some tacky mass wedding re-enacted by children. I was too hot and my head was muddled as the priest placed a small, thin disk of dry, flavourless bread on my tongue. I returned to my seat and a new panic overtook me, something they hadn't mentioned in the months of catechism lessons: should I chew the wafer or just let it dissolve? Chewing made the most sense; it was bread after all. But wasn't it disrespectful and probably blasphemous to chew the Body of Christ? So the wafer slowly turned to mush. And I sat there in the pew, no different than I had been before Communion, just a lot sweatier.

I can only imagine how happy I was to get home and take off that awful suit. And I can also imagine that even if you've never received communion sweating inside a polyester suit, you may be happy you don't have to wear a suit often, if ever, and that's a shame. Despite my experiences, I now love suits.

That said, there's a reason I put suits *after* jackets and trousers in this book. And it's not because of the practical reason that a suit is, after all, simply a jacket and trousers made of the same fabric, and once you've read those two previous chapters, you're pretty much set. It's not even because non-matching jackets and trousers will serve you well in both casual and formal occasions these days.

No, the reason is that the suit is waning, even fading from modern society. This has been prophesied before, for decades, in fact. But yet the suit is still around and still evolving. Suits were getting tighter and shorter a decade ago; they're filling out again in the here and now. But looking purely at the facts, fewer and fewer suits are being worn. And this is because the last bastions of the suit — corporate business, government, and TV journalism — are

Avoiding Black Suits

When I was getting married, and knew far less about clothing, I bought a suit at a large department store. I asked for a black suit because, you know, I was getting married and black is fancier, right? The salesman knew enough to warn me that black looks washed out and flat in natural light (one reason you only wear tuxedos *after dark*). Instead, he guided me toward midnight blue. Still dark, and therefore formal, blue has depth to it that makes it look much more attractive in natural or artificial light. I still offer up thanks to that salesman when I look at my wedding pictures. Too bad he wasn't there when I bought my square-toed shoes.

turning away from this symbol of power, prestige, and oversight. In some ways, I don't mind: folks in these fields never wore suits well, anyway. They often wore black suits, suits with sleeves and legs too long, or suits gaping around the neck. A whole series of abominations. But at least they kept the suit alive, and that matters, for me, because we have nothing to replace it. As goes the suit, so goes our global society's only symbol of formal occasion.

The lounge suit, as it used to be called, was not formal when it was first introduced. As the name suggests, it was for more casual endeavours. Over time, as the top end of formal wear started to fade — the frock coat, then white tie, then the tuxedo — the lowly suit moved up the formal ladder to the point where now a dark-blue suit is perhaps the most formal clothing most men own. But at least we have something, something to signify that a wedding or a funeral is in some way different, some way more special than a trip to the mall.

This is why I believe every man should own at least one suit: to give meaning, respect, and specialness to occasions. A dark-blue suit will serve a large number of occasions today, and not just weddings and funerals. Certain business events, special dinners, and even some job interviews will benefit from a sober, elegant, understated suit. And who knows, you might get called up to jury duty. And you don't want to do that in a hoodie and jeans.

Fabric

When it comes to the fit and construction of a suit, please revisit the previous sections on jackets and trousers. Originally, lounge suits were also referred to as "ditto" suits because the fabric was the same on the top and bottom. Nothing else is fundamentally different in how they are made or styled. Okay, the buttons are different, I'll give you that. On sport jackets, buttons often contrast the fabric, while on a suit, they are traditionally tone-on-tone with the suiting (the fabric used for making suits and jackets). And in many ways, it is the fabric that makes the suit.

FORMAL SUIT FABRICS

Wool is the established choice for a more formal business suit. It's funny but when, as a teenager, I first heard the term "wool suits," I imagined thick, heavy, tweedy flannel things. But wool is woven at so many weights, you can find anything from an almost light-as-air fresco, to a bulletproof tweed.

As is the case with other garments, the simpler and darker the fabric, the more formal. Midnight-blue worsted wool would be a good way to start if you're looking for something dressy yet versatile. As you introduce texture to the weave or pattern to the colour, the fabric becomes less formal. However, a dark pattern on a dark suit still retains formality while also adding a dash of personal style.

But fabric type, weave, and colour aren't the only factors that make a suit more or less formal. In general, the more shape (i.e., padding in the shoulders and chest) the more formal. The softer the suit, the more casual.

CASUAL SUIT FABRICS

"Casual suit" probably sounds like an oxymoron. After all, any suit today is seen as formal. But I do think there is a tiny sliver of space for something that straddles both ends. It's still a suit — jacket and trousers of the same fabric — but the specific fabric and the construction of the suit lessen its formality.

As mentioned, if you choose a wool weave that is more textured than smooth worsted, like a flannel or tweed, it is naturally less formal. Linen has a similar effect in summer: the wrinkles add an air of relaxation to the suit.

But for me, cotton is the main option when it comes to casual suits. It doesn't have the sheen of worsted wool, and since it can be a bit bulkier and wrinkly, it automatically looks less formal. The best example of this is corduroy. You'd never wear a corduroy suit into a board meeting, but I think with desert boots and an open collar shirt, a corduroy suit looks great out for dinner or at a movie. That said, I know that corduroy suits aren't for everyone. Like Wes Anderson movies: some people love them; some people hate them. Coincidentally, Wes Anderson wears corduroy suits all the time. And according to my non-scientific research, if you like his movies, you are more likely to wear corduroy suits.

FABRIC QUALITY

Assessing suiting is really no different from assessing fabric for jackets or trousers (see page 85 in "Sport Jackets" and pages 100–101 in "Trousers"). For example, some of the best fabrics come from England, France, and Italy, but that does not mean that every fabric from those countries is of high quality. You will still have to apply your standards of look and feel, regardless of which mill made the material. If you have your suit custom-made, you can sometimes rely on the tailor for advice, if they are actually making the suit. Made-to-measure salespeople may simply sell you the fabric that's best for themselves (fabric is often where custom makers have a better margin). Even getting to know a specific fabric mill isn't always enough, as larger mills produce varying qualities of fabric depending on the fabric's destination. Again, trust your eyes and your hand.

And don't get caught up with those "super" numbers. These refer only to the fineness of the fibres used and do not relate to quality. In fact, the quality of the fibres themselves is what matters because that is what will help the fabric hang better (drape), last longer, and look and feel better.

Style and Silhouette

The cut of a suit will greatly affect its perceived formality. The stiffer the jacket, the straighter the lines, the less ornamentation, the more formal. Logically, then, a soft-shouldered suit with generously curved lapels and patch pockets is far more casual than a square-shouldered, straight-lapelled, besom-pocketed suit.

Custom versus Ready-Made

A custom suit is not necessarily better than off-the-rack. While you may be able to select the features, influence the style, and be measured for a personalized fit, each of those steps can suffer from poor execution. In order to keep prices down, the maker might select inferior fabrics. Construction might be done in a sloppy or inconsistent way. Or measurements may be taken or communicated incorrectly. And even if all of those elements are correct, you and your tailor may not see eye to eye. Which means that even though technically the finished suit might be high quality, if you don't like it, if it doesn't "suit" you, the value is not there.

When it all does work together as it should, however, I get a huge value out of custom tailoring. And it isn't purely about the money in/garment out equation. A custom suit can be more than the sum of its parts.

Selecting the fabric is where building an ideal version of yourself begins. The tactile pleasure of feeling different weaves. Or taking a bolt of fabric, draped over your shoulder, right out of the store into the glare of daylight and passersby so that you can see if the colour is really right for you. This is why I so love buying fabric either in advance from a suiting supplier or from a tailor who still carries bolts of cloth. It's hard to drape a two-inch square sample of fabric around your body.

Then there's designing the suit, where I get to feel like an authority on style, and I can state, with conviction, that patch pockets are more rakish than flapped. All the while sipping espresso and talking with my tailor about style and life and Italy and all things elegant.

In the end, the garment is not just custom-made, not just unique to you. It has a story. It wasn't just made for you, it was made by you. (Metaphorically, of course. I can't stitch a seam to

Your First Suit

It is a cliché, but for good reason: your first suit needs to be as versatile as possible. You may end up owning only one, or it will be the one you go back to over and over. Either way, your first suit purchase is not the time to experiment or take chances (save that for your third or fourth). I highly recommend the traditional choice: dark-blue worsted wool, no pattern, two-piece, notch lapel, two-button front. And while I'd go for jetted pockets, to keep things understated, cuffs on the trousers are up to you. If you want to get even more life out of the suit and wear the jacket and trousers separately on occasion, swap the tone-on-tone buttons with dark-brown horn or bone. The jacket will look good on its own, while still looking subtle enough when part of the suit. And most importantly, steer away from high fashion; this is a suit you'll want to wear for years, not months. Choose cuts neither too tight nor too loose, too short or too long. Go for moderation in all elements, like the lapel width and shoulder silhouette. Try to picture yourself in as many situations as you can, and determine if it harmonizes with all of them.

save my life.) All of my custom suits — and shirts and jackets and trousers, for that matter — express who I am, and not just in their measurements.

Of course, a garment doesn't need to be custom-made to become a part of you. If you choose it carefully and with intent, if you wear it and care for it for many years, it will develop a life of its own. It will accrue memories, along with tiny specks of soy sauce and chicken grease. It will become, hopefully, an old friend. Or a beloved dog because, like a dog, a suit should be occasionally brushed (see "Caring for Your Wardrobe").

FINDING THE RIGHT TAILOR FOR YOU

The first time I commissioned a suit from a custom tailor I was so caught up in the romance of the process, I ended up with a garment that I only wore a few times before storing it in a basement closet. Technically, the suit fits and is well constructed, but the style and silhouette are wrong for me. I may have taken care in picking out the fabric, but I didn't apply that same care in choosing the tailor.

The first thing to consider when looking for a tailor is your image of yourself. For instance, you may want to bring along a photo of a suit you saw online or in a magazine, but you may not be aware that the model's body type is so unlike yours that the same suit wouldn't look as good on you. You may also think you are taller, shorter, thinner, or wider than you actually are, and try to design or compensate for that. Or you may have an idealistic image

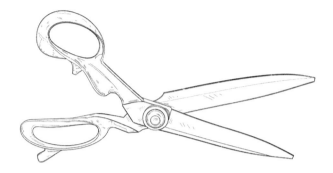

in your mind of the "perfect" suit and how it will transform you.

The other thing to consider is the tailor's own perspective. Chances are, they will see you as you really are, misshapen abnormalities and all. And their job is to make you look your best according to *their interpretation.* You may think you see eye to eye when you say you want a suit that is "not too slim." But the difference between your version of slim and that of the tailor might be in the magnitude of inches. Therefore, you need to be as specific as possible when discussing your vision for the suit. Keep in mind, however, that the tailor is looking at you through a lens of years or decades of training and working in a specific style and approach to tailoring.

And so the most important starting point when choosing a tailor is getting to know their style and approach. Look at as many examples of their tailoring as possible. Do their suits have the shoulder shape or the coat length or the lapel width you prefer? Do they hug the body or flow and drape around the chest and legs?

Are they light and unstructured or padded and shaped? Choose the tailor whose style best suits your own. If your styles aren't a match, don't try to impose a style on them. Attempting to push them toward a style that is not their own will, in my experience, leads to frustration and disappointment.

Commissioning a custom suit is about self-knowledge. It's about getting to know, after many years of experimentation and thought, what your personal style is all about — not to mention asking yourself what you need the suit for and what kind of lifestyle you lead. And finally, understand that a suit will not make you perfect but will, hopefully, make you feel like a better version of yourself.

Knitwear

A cardigan coat sweater of lightweight wool
and conservative color is a useful investment. It
can be worn without a coat on many occasions,
and has the advantage of being easily slipped
on without those arm-raising contortions
and the need to re-comb your hair.

— Cary Grant

I never travel anywhere without a sweater. I might be in Havana in the middle of a punishing heat wave and still, unused in my luggage, there will lie a folded merino wool cardigan. *Because you never know.* I think my obsession stems from being Canadian. I live in a cold country that occasionally gets warm and not the other way around. Although part of it, I like to think, comes from the sheer comfort of a good sweater. And that's something that anyone, almost anywhere, can appreciate.

Of all the garments in this book, knitwear is perhaps the one people associate most with its function: to keep you warm. And yet, as our culture becomes more and more casual, knitwear is moving from comfy home garment to general outerwear. But it should only do so if that knitwear is well made, fits well, and harmonizes with your outfit. In other words, you can replace a jacket with a lightweight pullover or cardigan, but not with your raggedy camping fleece — not if you are aiming for elegance. And therefore, you should put as much thought into your knitwear as you would into tailored outerwear.

Styles

A good sweater should last a lifetime. To do so, it must be well made, constructed of good materials, and cared for diligently (see "Caring for Your Wardrobe"). But it must also be, like all the items in this book, neither too in nor too out of fashion. That's why I rely on the classics: styles that have been around for decades, suggesting they should be around for a few more.

PULLOVER

Back when I was in grade ten, I bought a special sweater. It was to be my ticket into the popular set: a navy-blue crewneck made to imitate Shetland, so a bit fuzzy. I wore it, as I'd seen the popular kids do, with a white T-shirt underneath, just a bit showing at the neck. Despite my dislike for all things "preppy" at the time, I got the sweater in a desperate attempt to fit in, the winter uniform of the wannabe prep.

It didn't work. My popularity stayed rooted somewhere between zero and two friends. No new glances from girls were acquired. And sadly, for a couple of decades, in my mind an association was made with that type of sweater as "fashion over function."

A proper Shetland sweater, which I now own, is a marvel. Made on the Shetland Islands of northern Scotland, the silhouette is slim and flattering. The collar hugs your neck. It is impossibly warm and cozy. And the way it blurs your edges, literally, is almost anti-fashion.

But of course, this is only one type of pullover sweater. They can vary from thin merino to chunky cable knit. And while a crewneck can do wonders to a shirt collar, forcing it

Crewneck sweater

to attention like Beau Brummell's cravats of old, a V-neck is more relaxed, allowing a collar to lie more casually. Or, conversely, to draw attention to a tie. Or, God forbid, a T-shirt.

I have two types of pullover sweaters: heavier for warmth and as a top layer themselves; and lightweight, for layering, usually worn under a jacket. I don't have any V-necks, but I should remedy that at the first opportunity.

CARDIGAN

The other day, on returning home from a meeting, I was wearing a sport jacket and tie. After removing my oxfords and putting on my slippers, I removed my jacket and put on a cardigan. But kept the tie. I realized, at that moment, I had become Mister Rogers. Not a bad role model in the slightest. In my case, the resemblance may be only in sartorial habits, but I will continue to strive to be as saintly in all other facets of my life.

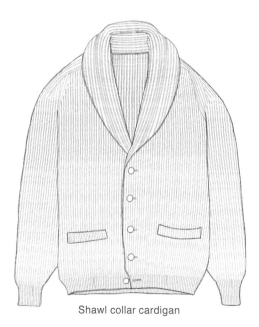

Shawl collar cardigan

To be fair, Mister Rogers always changed into sneakers (which I don't wear indoors) and his cardigans were the zippered kind (which I don't own).

But the point is that a cardigan is a more casual alternative to the sport jacket.

Again, the rule of texture also holds: the thicker/heavier the weave, the more casual the garment. So my heavy drop-shoulder shawl-collar cardigan never leaves my home and rarely sees guests. It's almost a bathrobe. My mid-weight, slimmer cardigans, on the other hand, serve as house jackets, while my lightweight cardigan is great for layering under a jacket or suit.

VESTS: PULLOVER OR BUTTON-UP

Sometimes a cardigan is too warm, especially when layered. This is all a game of a few degrees in temperature, isn't it? Trying to find just the right balance is especially challenging in the spring and fall when days start and peak at vastly different ends of the scale. That's when I suggest losing the sleeves.

All of my vests, whether pullover or button-up, are lightweight, ideal to wear under a jacket or even on their own.

The trick with vests, really, is length. Visually, the length of the vest determines the apparent size of the torso. A vest should always cover your waistband, but that should not determine its length. For instance, if you are wearing very high-waisted trousers, ending at the waist would give you a tiny looking chest, while low-waisted trousers would give you an abnormally long torso. Find the length of vest that best creates proportion with your body type (slightly longer if you have a short torso, slightly shorter if you have a

For an even more casual look when vested, try leaving the bottom *two* buttons of your vest undone — as long as this doesn't reveal your waistband. Hey, even the top button, too. Especially if it isn't too cold out.

Sleeveless cardigan/knitted vest

long torso) and simply don't wear a vest with low-waisted trousers. Actually, don't wear low-waisted trousers. That takes care of that.

Never fasten the bottom button of your button-up vest. This tradition comes originally from the vests of three-piece suits — and the rather corpulent King Edward VII, who couldn't do his up. As the story goes, in an attempt to make him comfortable, others followed suit, creating a trend. Or perhaps, as his grandson the Duke of Windsor claims, Edward VII just left the button undone by mistake. Regardless, there is also a functional reason not to complete the buttoning of a woven vest. I find that when a vest is buttoned up, the bottom is so tight that it can cause the vest to bunch up and mushroom out. Leaving the bottom button undone makes the vest look and feel more relaxed.

TURTLENECK

It takes chutzpah to wear a turtleneck. And not just because it goes in and out of fashion so violently. The turtleneck demands confidence because it puts your face on a pedestal, almost literally. You are completely covered, up to your chin, so everything becomes about your face. But hey, that's where people should be looking, anyway, right?

Plus, a turtleneck is practical. It keeps you warm from your chin to below your waist. It replaces a shirt, a collar, even a tie. Worn under a jacket or suit, it automatically conveys a casual, rakish spirit.

But be warned: the turtleneck is not without its pitfalls, the greatest being the neck roll itself. Too bulky and you look like you're in traction. Too loose and you appear to be about to pass out in hunger.

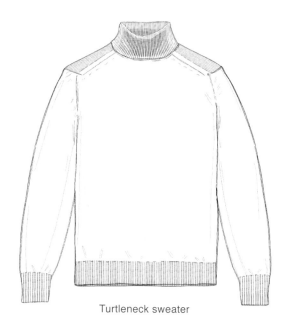

Turtleneck sweater

Fabric

The National Trust in Britain was recently faced with an existential challenge. Part of their mandate is to protect and watch over natural spaces and the health of the environment. That environment is being slowly polluted and choked by plastic and, specifically, micro plastics: the miniscule bits of fabric released from some types of clothes. Including fleece sweaters. Which are worn by National Trust staff.

What to do? Their idea was to call for new and better technology, to develop a fabric for their sweaters that was warm, durable, water resistant, and non-polluting. As is common today, they were looking to the future to solve a problem that had already been solved in the past. The solution is literally being paraded about many of Britain's parks and pastures: sheep's wool.

There is perhaps no better natural fibre in the world than wool. It is sustainable, naturally durable, and weather resistant, and when farmed compassionately, the ethics of the industry do not bother me. Wool is also incredibly versatile. It appears in so many other sections of this book: for suits, jackets, trousers, overcoats, socks, and glove linings. It can be woven and processed from super fine to super chunky.

TYPES OF WOOL

Wool is ideal for knitwear of all kinds, but it isn't as simple as just saying "get a wool sweater." Knitwear comes in a dizzying array of wool types. Here are the ones in my wardrobe alone:

NEW WOOL This is a catch-all phrase for any wool that has not been recycled or used in any way before being woven into a garment. This says little of the quality beyond that differentiator.

VIRGIN WOOL This is a tricky label as it can sometimes mean exactly the same thing as "new wool" but it can also refer to the wool that comes from a lamb's first shearing, which is extra soft and fine. This does still not connote quality, however, in and of itself.

LAMBSWOOL This is the proper name for the first wool sheared from a lamb. While it is among the softest, finest, and most flexible wool types, the name alone does not signify high quality.

MERINO WOOL Originally named after the type of sheep it is sheared from, merino wool is exceptionally fine, with long staples (a "staple" is a cluster of wool fibres), as well as being soft and flexible. It can be woven into remarkably lightweight knitwear while still being warm and cozy. The variety of grades of merino (like other types of wool, usually hidden from the customer) relate to the fineness of the fibres, not the quality.

GEELONG WOOL This wool comes from a specific type of merino sheep and can be as luxuriously soft and warm as high-quality cashmere. It has a shorter staple than merino, so it tends to produce a bulkier yarn. It is also more exclusive than other wools, which means knitwear made of Geelong can be more expensive. But, once again, this premium isn't necessarily connected to quality. However, it is unlikely a maker would use Geelong to create a substandard garment, unless the Geelong amount in the garment is overstated.

Cashmere

I don't have any cashmere sweaters in my wardrobe. Partially this is due to the high cost. But it's also because I am not primarily concerned with the type of wool, but where the sweater is made and the quality of construction. Plus, unfortunately, there's cashmere, and then there's *cashmere*. The market is flooded with garments labelled "cashmere" that do contain some wool from cashmere goats, but not all of it, or even much of it, is the prized long-staple belly hair. Instead, sheared shorter fibres from the rest of the goat are blended in. This produces a fabric that is not as soft or durable as the finest cashmere and, in terms of softness and durability, sits below average merino wool, for instance.

LABELLING WOOL

One of the reasons I keep harping on about wool types *not neces-sarily* signifying quality is because of poor labelling. In many coun-tries, a sweater can be labelled "merino wool" and contain only five percent merino, and not necessarily from actual merino sheep. The different types of wool can tell you something about how fine and soft they might be, but for quality, you're going to have to rely on your eyes and hands. And to a certain extent, price: fine wool sweaters just can't be had for cheap.

Fit

Knitwear can be mercifully forgiving when it comes to fit because, after all, it is not structured like a jacket or made of tightly wo-ven fabric like a shirt. But just like my advice elsewhere in this book, I choose not to go too loose or too tight. In fact, I let the weight of the weave decide for me: the lighter the weave, the more form-fitting, like merino pullovers and turtlenecks. The heavier the weave — like a chunky cardigan — the looser the fit. Other aspects of fit can be a bit relaxed with knitwear. For instance, there is a long tradition of drop-shoulder sweaters of all styles. Essentially, the body of the sweater is rather wide, so the shoulder seam sits a few inches down your arm. It's certainly not a look I'd want in my shirts, but as long as the fit in the body and sleeves is not too long, this look can add a relaxed touch.

Thinner woven knitwear is also perfect for layering. Whether a simple pullover or a buttoned vest, a thin piece of knitwear can add some colour and texture to a jacket and trousers or suit combination. Not to mention warmth. On the other hand, thinner knitwear can also replace almost all outerwear: a simple crewneck can look quite smart with a pair of flannel trousers. No need for a sport jacket.

Regardless of which fit you prefer, slim or loose, the shaping of the knitwear can be an indicator of quality. A quality maker will work from a pattern that creates a garment with a pleasing silhouette. If a new sweater has an odd shape — bulging under the arms, for instance — that is a sign that corners have been cut in the design process.

Construction

The best sweaters I own come from Britain and Italy and cost a fair penny. But that doesn't necessarily mean that every expensive British or Italian sweater is high quality. The way the knitwear is made provides some clues about quality.

Look at the finishing of the stiches. Unbutton the sweater or flip it inside out and look at the inside seams, especially the side seams and the back of the front placket (if it buttons up). They should be clean and smooth, not ragged and rough. Even a chunky sweater should have relatively slim, compact seams. A clean seam requires more time, patience, and skill to create.

Buttons can be a clue to quality. Are they shiny, cheap-looking plastic, or a natural material like bone, horn, or mother-of-pearl? Even if not, avoid sweaters with buttons that look subpar.

Assessing Quality

Despite what you may have heard, softness is not, in itself, a marker of quality wool. Some types of wool are simply softer than others. Softness can also lead to more pilling (see "Caring for Your Wardrobe" for how to deal with that), but perhaps counter-intuitively, pilling doesn't only happen on low-quality sweaters. It has more to do with the length of the fibres and wear patterns. Assessing quality in wool includes a number of factors, some of which can be hard to uncover as a customer. Clues to quality can be found in the types of wool used, as previously outlined. If, however, the knitwear is from Britain or Italy, you have a better chance of finding a quality garment — not a guarantee, but a good sign — because of a long tradition of craftsmanship and high standards of working conditions.

As with other garments in this book, ask the salesperson as many questions as you can; they should be able to tell you the type of wool used and where it was crafted. Designer brands are best avoided as they usually cut corners to justify their brand costs.

Overcoats

*Superficially, the prime function of the overcoat
is to protect its wearer from the cold, wind, dust
and rain. But it also demonstrates that he is on his
way somewhere. By putting on his overcoat, a man
indicates his intention to leave. By taking it off,
he indicates he has arrived.*

— Bernhard Roetzel

The automobile changed everything. It improved the mobility of a vast number of people. It influenced the layout and density of cities and towns around the world. And it upended the way we dress. In the 1950s and 60s, the car became our outer-wear. No more hats. No more galoshes. And no more overcoats.

A lot of other things happening in Western society during that time also contributed to this shift, most significantly the move away from formal tailored garments toward casual, sporty cloth-ing. Cumulatively, the result was the slow disappearance of the long, protective outer layer men had worn for decades. So much so that finding an overcoat today that is classic in proportion and design is a monumental task. But not impossible.

First, though, let's get our terms straight. The garment I'm talking about is a coat that is worn over other clothes such as a jacket, a suit, or heavy knitwear. It typically has a collar and lapel and can be single- or double-breasted. It can be more light-weight, often called a topcoat, or heavy, like a military greatcoat. Lengthwise, it can be as short as a sport jacket (which is impracti-cal for reasons explained below) or down to the ankles like a classic trench (which might be a bit too vampire-ish). However, I am not including various types of sportswear and other outerwear in this chapter, like field jackets and waxed cotton coats. While useful and stylish in their own ways, they are easier to find and more consist-ent in design, and therefore do not warrant special mention.

But if we are still a car-obsessed society, which we are, do we even need overcoats? Most department stores don't think we do, offering only a tiny selection of short coats that do little more than cover your torso. But despite how much time we spend in cars, a longer overcoat is still appreciated in climates where the tempera-ture drops below 0°C.

My family does not own a car, like more and more families today. I still spend a fair amount of time in taxis and rentals, but I certainly do more walking than my parents' generation did. And since I live in a city that experiences wind chill, a warm, protective overcoat is a necessity.

But I'm not kidding myself that this is all about function. If it were, I might just wear one of those sleeping bags with arms, the long puffy jackets you sometimes see on Premier League managers when temperatures in London drop to a frigid 2°C. No, a classic overcoat is also an expression of style and taste. The way the fabric hangs and moves with you, the pattern or colour, and the silhouette all contribute to an opportunity to express personality and taste.

Avoid Synthetic Winter Coats

While they may be warmer than the average wool overcoat, synthetic coats come at a real cost, and that cost is usually environmental. They are mostly made of petroleum, after all. Their manufacture involves chemicals and pollutants, they cannot be easily mended or altered, and when they reach the end of their life (which is invariably short because of the previous point), they are doomed to sit in a landfill for God knows how long until their plastic constituent parts return to their natural liquid state.

While natural fibres may not be as insulating as modern synthetic fabrics, try this time-tested solution: layering. With enough warm layers under your overcoat, you can manage very well in very frigid weather. Generations before us have.

Style

You have a few key style decisions to make when adding an overcoat to your wardrobe. Single- or double-breasted is a big one. While double-breasted does provide more insulation, literally doubling the fabric up front, it can look more formal. Length is another consideration. Today, most ready-made overcoats barely cover the seat which, while fashionable and easier to get in and out of a car with, is practically useless in cold weather, when exposed thighs can get so painful. My advice is to focus on your knees: I'd recommend a coat that ends just above or just at the knee. But be aware that even that little bit of fabric, just a few inches, has a huge visual impact. I find that an overcoat that ends below the knee can give the impression of being cape-like.

Another consideration is shoulders. A softer shoulder is more casual looking than a built-up shoulder. Considering that an overcoat will usually go over a jacket that might already have shoulder padding, I would recommend minimum padding on an overcoat to avoid looking like an American football player.

Fit

Overcoat silhouettes have always followed jacket styles as fashions fluctuated over the last hundred years. In the early twentieth century, they were, like jackets, full and oversized. By the 1920s in America, the shoulders had narrowed, reflecting soft-shouldered jackets. Due to the recent fashion for tight, short suits, stores are stocked with tight, short overcoats. In this sense, fashion has gone too far, making overcoats all but useless in their task: to keep you warm and protected. We have to find a balance between a contemporary silhouette and function. I lean toward the latter.

However, something to understand when shopping — regardless of fashion — is that overcoat sizes are traditionally based on what you wear under them. So if you, like me, wear a size 42 sport jacket, you'd wear a size 42 overcoat, even though it measures bigger than forty-two inches in the chest. Which is why it's essential when trying ready-to-wear overcoats to also be wearing a jacket of some sort underneath.

This also helps determine how the overcoat fits in general. Is there enough space in the sleeves for your jacket to fit comfortably? Do the sleeves of the overcoat extend past the sleeves of your jacket but not all the way to your knuckles? Does the overcoat length cover the length of your jacket? If there are shoulder pads, do they create too much bulk for your liking? Beyond that, it is a personal preference whether you like a longer or shorter coat, bulkier or slimmer. Again, long and loose means more warmth, and you'll thank me for that when it's twenty below and the wind is blowing like a banshee.

Features to Look For

As with knitwear, when assessing an overcoat look at the buttons. Natural horn or bone are always preferable to plastic. Another often-overlooked feature is the glove pocket. This large interior pocket is perfectly placed to store your gloves when you come in from the cold, and its inclusion is a sign of a maker who goes beyond just the basics.

Fabric

As with the other garments in this book, I recommend 100 percent natural fabrics. And when it comes to overcoats, the best choice is wool. It is naturally warm, insulating, and water resistant. It is also sustainable and mendable. And caring for your wool overcoat is as simple as the occasional brushing (and very rare dry cleaning).

However, if you are looking for a lighter-weight overcoat, specifically for rain, such as a trench coat or mackintosh, then cotton is the way to go. And for over a century, mostly British weavers have found ways of making cotton that is water repellent, like rubberized or Ventile cottons, without resorting to synthetic fabrics.

Types of Overcoats

What follows is just a small sample of the many styles of overcoats available. But these are some of the overcoat styles I have worn and recommend.

RAGLAN/BALMACAAN

A good friend from Newfoundland once told me that back home "raglan" means overcoat. Which speaks to how pervasive this soft-shouldered overcoat is in northern European, rural cultures. Raglan refers to the sleeves, which attach to the collar rather than the shoulder (there is no shoulder seam on a raglan coat). So a number of different types of overcoats can have raglan sleeves. My favourite, and the one I own, is the balmacaan.

Originally from Scottish country life, the balmacaan is naturally casual. It is loose and soft, a working coat. If made in a heavy tweed, it manages to look classic and contemporary at the same time. Mine is quite large, which is traditional, but modern versions fit closer to the body. Just remember: if the fit is too close, there's not enough space for air to get trapped and create an extra layer of warmth, thus making the coat a glorified windbreaker.

Structure of a raglan sleeve

Traditional
pea coat

PEA COAT

Probably the best combination of classic style, functionality, modernity, and ease of purchase on this list is the pea coat. But be warned: they have not been able to avoid the disastrous effects of the fashion world. If you want a classic, original-style pea coat, your best bet might be a military outfitter or surplus store.

By "classic" I mean heavy navy or mid-blue wool, wide double-breasted lapels, length that covers the seat, and six tone-on-tone buttons. Things to avoid: black fabric (there are enough black winter coats in the world), short (what's the point?), and anchor buttons (unless you're ten years old).

DOUBLE-BREASTED

Light grey, in a wool/cashmere blend, with peak lapels and slash pockets: this is my most formal overcoat. Partially, this is due to the peak lapels, but the length and structured shoulders also make this coat better over a jacket and tie or even my tuxedo, than anything more casual. As such, I don't wear it often but I do love having a more formal yet warm option.

TRENCH COAT

I guess I've always been drawn to classic style because when I was a teenager, I copped Bogart's look of long double-breasted tan trench coat and fedora hat. But I was also clueless, so I wore these over jeans and tie-dyed T-shirts. Looking back, I don't regret my desire to dress in a classic way. It's just too bad no one in my life could offer me guidance, suggesting, perhaps, that I dial back the overcoat and hat while ramping up the trousers and shirts.

This is still an inherent tension in dressing today, and the trench coat is the perfect symbol. The classic trench I wore as a teenager is so associated with an era that to wear it now, unironically, is almost impossible. Which is a shame because it works so well to keep you warm and dry. But with a few adjustments to the original, a trench can still be worn without looking like a pretentious teenager.

First, I would lose some of the accoutrements, like the shoulder epaulettes and many of the extra buckles and belts. But keep the double-breasted construction, wide lapels, and length to the knee, which add not only function but also style. Second, colour: instead of the typical tan (which can show dirt easily), darker colours, like navy blue, muted green, or a mid-grey or mid-brown, are perhaps more elegant. And third, if you're going to wear it with a hat (which makes sense if you're trying to keep warm and dry) make sure the hat contrasts with the colour of your coat. Otherwise your ensemble can look like a costume.

Assessing Quality

Since most overcoats are, in a sense, just longer versions of sport coats, you can assess them with similar criteria: by looking closely at the fabric, the construction, and the silhouette.

First, trust your hands and eyes when it comes to the fabric: does it feel robust, with some bounce, while looking dense? In other words, does it feel good to the touch? Second, are the seams, inside and out, clean, even, and carefully applied? And third, does the jacket sit well on your shoulders? Since the overall silhouette can vary depending on overcoat style, make sure the shoulders have a look — soft or structured — that is pleasing to you.

Beyond the objective markers of quality is the personal appreciation of value: how does the overcoat make you feel? I don't just mean warm or protected, formal or casual. It should make you feel like you're going somewhere. And that you mean it.

Socks

Socks should be luxurious and in good repair.
Actually, socks are one of the cheapest items to
which the idea of luxury can be attached.
A fifty-dollar pair of socks can make you
feel like a million bucks.
— Glenn O'Brien

I am going to bet that of all the garments you wear, especially the ones you wear the most, you think about socks the least. Perhaps they are functional at worst, "funky" at best. Or they are simply disposable, something you go through so quickly you barely give them a thought. And yet of all the garments in this book, no other common item is as overlooked while also being as important — to you and your wardrobe — as quality hosiery. You know, socks.

First and foremost, you should invest in socks because of the physical joy and pleasure of wearing something well made, of having good-quality fabric against your skin. The first time I slipped on a pair of *not* dirt-cheap socks, I immediately felt, as Glenn O'Brien says, like a million bucks. The way they followed the contours of my feet and ankles without bunching up; the lack of heavy seams at the toes; the coziness and comfort in their embrace.

Another important reason to invest time and money in your socks is that they can be the weakest link in your wardrobe. Because they might be overlooked, and therefore bunching at your ankles, that flash of colour and texture when you walk or sit down can undo the rest of your hard work in putting together an outfit.

Maybe because we don't see them much or we're so used to wearing poor quality, socks are often an oversight. They are also the most disposable item of a classic wardrobe, lasting less time than other items, so maybe it doesn't seem worth the effort. But let me assure you, it most certainly is. Like all other aspects of a wardrobe, once you have experienced quality socks, you can't really go back to buying them ten at a time in a plastic bag.

I think about my socks the same way I think about the rest of my wardrobe: in terms of fit, construction, quality, and style. Instead of simply "dark" and "dressy," you can express so much more with your socks without having to take the ham-fisted route of "fun socks." Personally, I like to have fun with everything I'm wearing, and I want each piece to express my mood and personality. But I don't like to shout about it.

Colour

I stick with solids or minimally patterned socks in dark, classic colours with my tailored or more formal clothes. You can never go wrong with navy, for instance, which, while dark, has more depth than black. And there's no need to think of sombre colours as limiting. Forest green and burgundy can be quite striking while still remaining understated, particularly when combined with grey flannel trousers and brown oxfords. Subtle patterns like low-contrast stripes or a micro-houndstooth can also be quite elegant.

In summer or with more casual outfits I might try earthy tones, beige and mossy green, but I abandoned bright colours some time ago. They just feel showy.

Of course, sock colour depends on your personal sense of style as well as your wardrobe. Not to mention your culture and your concept of masculine style. In France, for instance, I saw a fair amount of brightly coloured socks — partially because bright colours are seen as masculine there, allowing for bursts of flamboyance. But when it comes to theories about colour and ostentation in masculinity, that's a whole other book.

I don't pay too much attention to the rule that your socks should be the same colour as your trousers. The idea is that matching these elements lengthens your legs because the colour visually extends from your trousers. Supposedly, wearing socks the same colour as your shoes does the opposite, extending your feet and shortening your legs. I have never felt this is true at all times and for everyone, so I loosen up and go with colours that harmonize with my trousers or shoes, perhaps picking up on a colour from my shirt, tie, or pocket square. I don't like a lot of contrast, but as long as there's a tonal balance, I don't sweat it.

Material

The fundamental ingredient for quality in socks is the yarn used. You simply cannot make high-quality socks out of poor or mediocre materials. Unfortunately, labels do not go into enough detail explaining the quality of the yarn used to weave the socks. Like with other garments, you must do a bit of research to find out if the manufacturer is using quality materials. One sign of quality on a label, however, is "Cotton Lisle" (also *Fil d'Écosse*). This is a superior type of cotton both for its long staple and its processing. More on that in a moment.

And even though I would urge you to stick with 100 percent natural fibres, a mix of synthetics in socks does have its place, unlike in the other garments in this book. A small amount of nylon or elastane, for durability and comfort, sometimes cannot be avoided, as long as these components are in the minority.

WOOL

Perhaps the warmest option, wool socks don't necessarily only come thick and bulky, if that's what you're picturing. But even fine merino wool socks will wear warm, so I reserve them for winter months. Make sure to wash wool socks with extra care (see "Caring for Your Wardrobe").

COTTON

The best option for all-weather socks is cotton. It wears both warm in winter and cool in summer, is naturally comfortable and durable, and washes easily. The best cotton I've found, which combines those factors with a price that is approachable, is Cotton Lisle. Its extra-long fibres make this type of cotton special and worth seeking out. Extra-long staple cotton is pretty much what the name says: cotton made up of fibres that are much longer than regular cotton. And that matters because when the cotton is processed, and then mercerized, the length means less overall breakage.

Now, to be completely honest, cotton can be nasty for the environment. It requires an awful lot of water to grow (which could be otherwise used for food crops or drinking). And the processing, specifically the mercerizing and dying of the cotton, is chemically intensive. However, as with many other aspects of the classic wardrobe, much of this impact can be

Mercerizing is a process that uses caustic soda (also called sodium hydroxide or lye) to swell and straighten cotton fibres, permanently making them smoother and giving them a silk-like lustre. It also greatly increases their durability, preventing the fibres from shrinking or tearing.

minimized by getting as much out of your clothes as possible. Specifically, the environmental impact of mercerizing cotton is offset by its durability — as long as you don't eat up energy by tumble drying, which you never should (as discussed in "Caring for Your Wardrobe").

LINEN

My go-to material for summer socks is linen. Not only is it super breathable and light-wearing, it wicks away moisture. And we sweat a lot through our feet. An awful lot. I find linen so comfortable that over the past few summers, I have found I prefer over-the-calf linen socks to being bare-ankled. I know it sounds counterintuitive, but perhaps the moisture wicking and breathability does it. Or the "I can't believe I'm wearing socks" feeling compensates for the extra degree of temperature. Either way, when I'm dressed a bit more formally in the summer, nothing beats linen. The only drawback is durability. Linen wears through faster than cotton, in my experience. But that's not such a problem once you know how to darn your socks (see "Caring for Your Wardrobe").

SILK

Known for its luxuriously soft feel and shimmery look, silk is remarkably good at keeping your feet warm in winter and cool in summer. However, since it requires more care in washing and can be so sheer as to show the skin through the material, I only have one pair of silk socks: to wear with my tuxedo. They make the experience of wearing black tie feel even more special.

Fit

One great advantage of moving to better quality socks is better sizing. Like other wardrobe essentials, avoid anything marked "small," "medium," or "large." One size fits none. Instead, look for a specific shoe-size range, and the smaller the range the better. For instance, socks listed in sizes 9–10, instead of sizes 7–11.

I prefer a sock that fits slightly tighter than looser. And the fit at the heel is paramount. Like a good shoe, the heel of a sock should shape around your contours, with no resulting bunching up above the heel. I would recommend trying one pair from a number of different companies first — wash and wear each a number of times — until you find a sock that fits well, feels good, and lasts, then stick to that maker.

However, if a specific maker's socks don't fit you well, that doesn't necessarily mean they are poor quality. So many elements are involved in shaping and constructing socks, and our feet are all such different shapes and sizes, that a perfect fit is almost impossible.

A Good Fit

There are two basic ways that sock makers attempt to create a good fit. One is to add elastane or nylon to the socks so that the extra stretch accommodates individual contours. However, this is a compromise that lowers the natural yarn's comfort and breathability. The other method is to make the socks on machines with a higher number of weaving needles. This means more knitting points — literally more stitches — which makes the socks more elastic. While the result is never as stretchy or durable as synthetic blends, the benefit is retaining the qualities of the natural yarn.

Length

Now, here is where this section becomes controversial: should you go mid-calf or over the calf (what some shops snobbishly call "executive")?

I am firmly in the over-the-calf camp because either I want to show off my legs or I don't. In summer, with loafers and casual pants, yes, it's all about the bare ankles. But if I'm wearing socks,

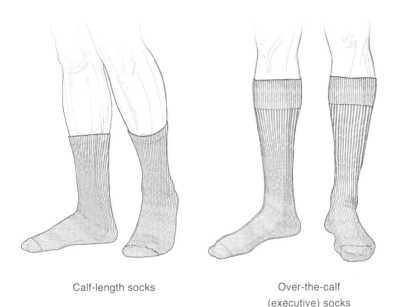

Calf-length socks

Over-the-calf
(executive) socks

then I'm wearing socks. The problem with calf-length socks, of course, is their inability to stay up all day long. And I just can't stand the discomfort of bunched up socks or how sloppy they look. I could recommend sock garters — you know, those elastic straps you see in black and white movies that fit at the top of your calves and hold up socks — but that might be a bridge too far. Then again, without garters you end up with bunched up socks, revealing unsightly hairy calves when you sit or cross your legs. When you're dressed more formally, in a jacket or suit for instance, this moment of sloppiness can undo all the work you've put into the rest of your appearance.

Construction

Socks aren't that complicated to make, especially compared to shoes and jackets. However, there are two key areas where the construction speaks to a higher level of craftsmanship and quality: the top and the bottom.

Socks are woven as tubes, which means the end, the toe, needs to be closed, a process that happens separately from the weaving. Large-scale, industrial sock makers will simply cut and sew the ends closed, producing a thick seam along the toe of each sock. This method is both uncomfortable — as it pushes against your toes when wearing shoes — and unsightly. Higher-quality makers, using the same thread as the socks, instead link the end points together, loop by loop, creating a thin seam. While this used to be done by hand, more and more it is a mechanical process, but still one that requires investment and skill, thus raising the cost of the socks.

The other sign of quality construction is found at the other end of the socks, and this specifically applies to thinly woven, dressier socks. There are typically two different regions at the tops of socks: the

Roughly cut and stitched toe seam vs carefully linked toe seam

main tube of the sock and then a two- to five-inch band right at the opening. You can see that this band is woven differently, tighter, to create the tension needed to hold up the socks. But on higher-quality socks, this region actually has two weaves: a strip at the very top and another between this top strip and the body of the socks that are woven at different tensions. This allows the socks to better shape over your calves without the top region having to be extra tight.

Durability

Of course, one of the big issues with socks is how long they last. And again, like a good-quality tailored wardrobe, socks require special care that can help them last longer (see "Caring for Your Wardrobe"). Even when socks are reinforced with synthetic fibres, they will break down at the key points of friction: the toe, the ball, and under and behind the heel. Darning will give socks a second life, but even the finest socks in good repair will eventually degrade to such a state they must be replaced, often faster than the rest of your wardrobe.

But this is not a reason to spend less time and money on hosiery. As someone in the sock business explained to me, it's a question of what you value: natural-fibre socks will not last as long as synthetic blends, but for the time they do last, they will breathe better and feel more comfortable. Or, as another friend told me: "A bottle of wine that is more expensive will not fill more glasses. It is just better."

While price and brand are not always guarantees of quality, good socks simply cannot be had for cheap.

Gloves

I employed three tradesmen to make my gloves —
one for the hand, a second for the fingers,
and a third for the thumb!
— Edward Bulwer-Lytton,
Pelham, or Adventures of a Gentleman

Gloves can transform your hands as shoes can transform your feet. A good pair of gloves — that fit well and are expertly crafted of good materials — are not only warm and comfortable, they can immediately elevate your look. For such a small item, gloves add a disproportionate amount of elegance, sharpness, and personality to an outfit. It took me a long time to figure this out.

I used to feel, like many people, that gloves were essentially disposable. Either they didn't last long or you'd lose one or both. Who cared? So you invested neither much thought nor much money into them. This, however, is exactly what large, global brands want us to think. With glove sales shrinking in the 1980s as wardrobes continued their seemingly ever-downward spiral of casualness, large companies hit upon a solution: instead of selling a few pairs of fine, quality gloves, sell more pairs of cheap, flimsy gloves. Make them inexpensive enough, and people would return to buying gloves. Make them disposable, and you'd have an endless market. Sadly, as with so many other garments in our wardrobes, not only does this lead to excessive amounts of pollution and waste, it's another lost opportunity to have a deeper connection to our clothes through garments we actually care about, garments that grow old with us.

For generations, people used to get good gloves and take care of them. You would only have a pair or two, but they were an essential part of your wardrobe. And you made sure to take the extra care to not lose one or both. Overcoats, as mentioned earlier, were even made with inner pockets to help hold on to fine gloves.

Today, most stores are filled with poor or mediocre gloves. Made with synthetic or low-grade leather in sizes that fit no one well, it's no wonder gloves don't fill people with inspiration. But there are excellent gloves to be found, and when you do find them, when you put them on for the first time — the fabric shaping to the contours of your fingers, thumb, and palm; the comforting feel of a fine lining; the smell of quality leather — you almost never want to take them off.

Gloves versus Gloves

Just to be clear, I'm not talking about workwear-style, winter, deep-warmth gloves. While I do want my gloves to keep me warm while looking elegant, I have separate pairs for shovelling the snow or walking the dog, made of heavier leathers and some synthetic materials. However, I didn't want to call this chapter "dress gloves" for fear of evoking an image of white silk, top hats, and monocles.

Colour

You won't find many rules or sweeping proclamations in this book. But here's one: don't wear black gloves.

It's a hard ask, I know, because almost every store in Canada and the U.S. stocks only black gloves. There are a number of reasons for this: an anachronistic feeling of formality in black; the idea that black is somehow easier to care for and goes with anything; and because most businessmen wear black shoes. While those sentiments may hold some truth, black has little character or personality. Especially when compared to all the options available.

Glove colour was traditionally influenced by the colour of your shoes. Since so many men in Canada and the U.S. used to wear nothing but black leather shoes, we had a surplus of black gloves.

But now that we are discovering — like the Italians did generations ago — the personality and possibilities of brown shoes, I would hope our gloves will follow suit.

> Don't worry too much about matching your gloves and your shoes. Brown and brown, sure, but the tones don't have to be exact. That would be too on the nose, too precise. Dressing should be a joy, not a deference to rules.

I'll admit, when I first decided to liberate my hands from the sartorial oppression of black gloves, I jumped to the polar opposite. While visiting Florence a few years ago, I tracked down a tiny glove shop I'd read about on the internet, one of the only glove makers left in the lovely city. And I knew exactly what I wanted, as I had also read about them online: unlined yellow peccary gloves.

Back in the 1930s — often referred to as the golden age of menswear — yellow gloves were *de riguer*. Despite what black and white photos might have us believe, people, especially fashionable men, wore a lot of colour. Inspired by this, I picked up a pair of the dashing yellow gloves. I chose an unlined pair — literally just the leather, no wool or other lining — and made of peccary because it was the most historical and authentic. Plus, it's such a unique leather, thin with the distinctive spotted pattern of the pig-like mammal's hide.

Alas, I rarely wear the gloves. The thinness means they are perfect for about two weeks a year where I live, when the weather is just a bit too cool to go bare-handed, but not cold enough to require serious warmth. And while I love the colour aesthetically, the gloves do make me look a tad jaundiced. Perhaps this is why yellow fell out of favour.

But there is no shame in taking chances with your wardrobe. In fact, sometimes it's like tuning in to a radio station using an old dial: you need to go a little past the station to make sure you're getting the best signal. However, as I've advised elsewhere in this book, don't do what I did: your first pair of fine leather gloves shouldn't be an experiment. I highly recommend the more sober and, in my opinion, useful choice, which is brown.

Peccary leather pattern

I prefer a brown that is neither dark nor light for general wear. It goes with practically anything and will develop a nice patina with age. If you wear black shoes, then you can go with a deep, dark brown.

There are plenty of other colours out there, including grey, dark blue, and green, but I get so much pleasure and versatility from brown, and the variety of leathers is so vast, that I'm sticking to the elegant route. I still have the yellow gloves, by the way, because I do love them, but I only wear them when I'm feeling particularly flamboyant.

Fit and Sizing

It's hard to find a glove that "fits like a glove." This is because, like all ready-made clothing, pre-existing sizes are approximations. They fit nobody perfectly. While gloves in a size 8.5 fit my palm and middle finger, there is usually a bit of space above my pinky. But

Different Gloves for Different Hands

Don't be too put off if a pair of gloves fit slightly differently on each hand. Not only is it impossible to make gloves identical — due to the fact that each piece of leather cannot be stretched absolutely the same — but, like feet, our hands are not always exactly the same sizes. Try to find a balance while ensuring that the fit on your dominant hand is best.

I've learned to not be too concerned if gloves do not fit perfectly on each finger. That said, leather gloves should be quite snug when you first put them on. As long as the length is good in the fingers, they should fit snugly around the fingers, the palm, and the wrist. They will stretch slightly as you wear them and hopefully, over time, stretch to your hand shape. Gloves that fit snugly at the wrist, without the use of elastic or a strap, are something to look for because that fit speaks of better leather, pattern, and construction.

Also, I look at the fit around my thumb. Does the glove contour, or is there extra fabric between my thumb and other fingers when my glove is extended? The closer the glove sits to the base of all my fingers, the better. I also prefer that my gloves don't end just past my palm but extend a couple of inches, covering my wrist. My one pair of gloves that only extend an inch or so often leave exposed skin. Not a good feeling when it's below zero.

And just like my advice on socks, avoid gloves that come in "small," "medium," and "large." Sizes in half increment numbers allow for a greater fine tuning of the pattern, allowing for better fit. Quarter sizes are, of course, the best, but can be extremely hard to find. Regardless, since the size number is based only on the circumference of your palm, it is always important to try different makers' gloves as there might be differences in how they fit your particular fingers.

Materials

As with other garments, the quality of materials used, in this case leather, contributes in a big way to the overall quality of the gloves. This is because the leather should stretch to fit better over time. Quality leather is durable and will last for years to come. And it will do so nicely, developing a patina as time passes. However, it is unlikely that the label will tell you much about the quality of the leather. For that, you will have to rely on trusted sellers and your own research about different makers, who are increasingly transparent about their process.

Within the range of leather gloves, there is a wide variety of types.

GENUINE LEATHER Avoid. As discussed in the section "Leather Shoes," this is a processed leather product where bits and pieces left over from creating top grain and full grain leathers are combined and reconstituted to produce "genuine leather." It will not age well and is not very durable.

LAMBSKIN This leather is to gloves what box calf is to shoes: a good starting point in terms of quality. It tends to be soft and durable with a simple, plain finish.

DEERSKIN A more standard glove leather, deerskin has a grain and is thicker than hairsheep.

HAIRSHEEP I know it sounds weird, and before researching gloves I didn't know this was a thing, but there's a type of sheep in parts of Africa that grows hair, not wool. And its hide produces a leather that is perfect for thin, dressier gloves. The leather has a smooth look, while being flexible and durable.

PECCARY This mostly wild, pig-like South American mammal produces perhaps the best leather for gloves. It is soft, durable, warm, and distinctive. The spotted pattern can't be missed. But since the slaughter of these animals is tightly controlled, this leather is more exclusive and thus more expensive. (Very similar to peccary is carpincho, a leather from a large South American rodent.)

Lining

As with almost everything else in this book, I suggest sticking with 100 percent natural fabrics for your glove linings. Two of the best I've found are wool and cashmere. The latter feels more luxurious, of course, but that comes at a cost if it is true, high-quality cashmere.

Sadly, there are now many grades of cashmere, never labelled distinctly, so simply seeing that word does not guarantee quality (see page 126 in "Knitwear"). Meanwhile, wool does a perfectly good job of keeping you warm and dry for a more reasonable cost.

Extra thickness in your lining will, of course, provide extra warmth, but the trade-off is silhouette. Silk lining means gloves that are thin and feel luxurious when you put them on. But they do little to keep you warm. In terms of lining colour, almost anything is available but I tend to stick to tone-on-tone with the gloves themselves, usually beige for a mid-brown glove. I have one pair with red lining, but I regret the choice: it's a flash of colour at the wrist when I don't always want it.

Construction

The quote that opens this chapter is from a satirical novel about an obsessed dandy, but it's not as ridiculous as it may seem. Gloves are, in some ways, like a pair of trousers with five legs. Only far more active. A remarkable amount of engineering and craft is involved in making a pair of gloves that not only fit well when you first slip them on, but continue to do so as you live in them.

A lot of that comes down to how the leather is prepared. Before cutting and sewing, the leather on quality gloves is first stretched. It is difficult to tell, on a new pair of gloves, if the leather has been well stretched or stretched at all, but leather that has been stretched properly will age and contour to your fingers better and be more durable.

Beyond the leather used and the skill involved in cutting and sewing together gloves, something else that sets high quality apart from low is the pattern used to create them. An expertly drafted pattern will help create a glove that not only contours well to your hand but presents a pleasing silhouette.

Assessing Quality

As with other garments in this book, assessing quality at the time of purchase is a tough job. Over time, as you get to know leather better and as you find out more about makers that are known for quality, it will get easier. But to start with, here are some things to look out for.

First and foremost, for non-suede gloves, the leather should feel soft, almost like your skin, neither too dry nor too greasy. The leather should also not look perfect, without any sign of grain or blemishes of any kind. That lack of character can mean the leather has been treated in some way, has not been stretched, or has not been stretched well.

In terms of the stitching, as with other garments, look closely at the inside of the glove to see how much care has been taken with the finishing. However, hand stitching (a look that can be faked) is not necessarily a sign of quality. Better a glove be stitched well by machine than stitched poorly by hand.

And finally, but just as important, how does the glove fit? If it wraps around the contours of your hand and wrist, producing a lovely silhouette, that is usually a result of quality in all other aspects of leather and construction.

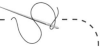

Stitching Styles

Two styles of stitching greatly impact the look of the gloves. They are either stitched while the glove is inside out so that when they are flipped, the stitches disappear inside the glove, producing a dressier, smoother outline; or the stitching is done on the outside of the glove, resulting in a more casual, sporty look, with clearly outlined fingers. One is not superior to the other in terms of quality — that really comes down to the quality of the stitching itself. It's just a choice based on personal preference.

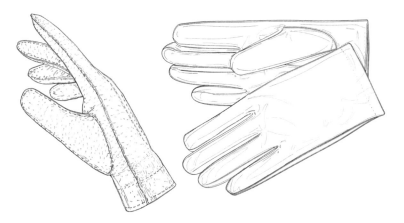

Peccary glove with
external stitching

Lambskin leather gloves with
internal stitching

Dress Hats

If you are a boy, you must wear a cap. If you are a man, you must wear a hat.
— Glenn O'Brien

My love of dress hats began when I was a teenager. I'll admit there was a heavy dose of nostalgia for old movies, mixed with a total lack of style. So I ended up wearing a cheap fedora, a trench coat, tie-dyed T-shirts, and jeans. Yes, I was that guy. But as the years went on and I learned more about hats and developed my own sense of style, I grew to appreciate all the ways a great hat can elevate a look and finish off an outfit. The curving sweep of a brim or the asymmetrical shape of a crown. The stylish interplay between the hat's colour and its ribbon. And most importantly, the feeling I get from wearing a hat. In an excellent hat, I feel that I'm fully dressed, that I'm sure of myself, that I'm a grown-up.

But I won't ignore the elephant in the room that's making you think about skipping this chapter: most men don't wear hats anymore. And chances are you've decided you don't look good in hats. But consider this: do you think all those guys, in most Western cities in the 1930s and 40s, thought they looked dumb in hats? Of course not. But that's not the real issue here. The issue is that you look *different* in a hat.

The sad truth is that conformity has an enormous impact on how we dress. Most men don't wear hats because other men don't wear hats. That said, a few years ago, on my first visit to Milan, all it took was seeing a number of guys, every day, wearing what Italians call "Borsalinos" to make me feel a lot less self-conscious. For once, I wasn't the only one on the street in a hat. The funny thing is, you can get this feeling on your own. Once I started wearing hats regularly, I grew accustomed to the way I looked in a hat and it felt completely normal and natural. In fact, it now feels weird to leave the house without something on my head.

So why don't most men wear hats anymore (except for the Italians)? First, starting in the 1950s, Western society became far more casual than it had ever been. Formality in everyday dress started to fade away, replaced by a wardrobe dominated by one garment: jeans. This was also part of a cultural movement of rebellion

What Are "Dress Hats"?

This category of hats includes a whole range that go by many names such as fedora, trilby, homburg, pork pie, and so on. What they all share is a blocked (shaped) oval crown — the top of the hat, which is then often further shaped with creases and dents — and a brim that goes all the way around. The brim can be wide, narrow, curved, rolled, or edged with fabric. These hats can be stiff or soft, though most contemporary dress hats are on the softer side. Most dress hats have a ribbon around the bottom of the crown which can be tall or narrow, of various colours, and preferably made of silk. Ribbons are also adorned with some kind of bow treatment, from simple to fancy knots and, occasionally, feathers on more sporty hats.

that included a growing concern among men for hairstyles. But here's the thing: dress hats are just that — hats meant to be worn with *dressier* clothing. Overcoats and ties and oxfords. Not biker jackets, T-shirts, and engineer boots.

The second big reason a lot of men stopped wearing hats was not their wardrobe or rebellious nature. It was the automobile. As we observed in the "Overcoats" section, the car became outerwear starting in the 1950s. I've heard many stories of fathers who would leave the house with a hat on, only to throw it in the back seat of the car when they got in. And there the hat would remain, rarely worn again. It just wasn't essential anymore.

It's also for practical reasons that I want to make a case for wearing dress hats. Other than an umbrella, almost nothing does a better job of protecting your head, face, and neck from harmful sun or miserable rain and snow than a brimmed hat. I find it particularly amusing that in this day and age, when I think most people would argue their clothing choices are based on practicality, there are so many uncovered heads out there. I know, I sound like your mom. But you know what? She's right.

Beyond that, if you're going to wear suits and jackets and overcoats, even occasionally, what will you wear on your head? On a cold day, a guy in a big, comfy overcoat looks unfinished, and fundamentally unwise, walking around with a bare head. A baseball cap worn with a suit would look as out of place, I'd argue, as a fedora worn on a baseball diamond.

But I get it. With so few dress hats out there, you draw attention to yourself by wearing one. But that's just the point. In the same way you shouldn't be shy about proclaiming your sense of personal style and elegance with your shoes or jacket, you can wear a hat with confidence. Almost every time I wear a dress hat, someone comments not only on how good I look but about how they wish they could wear hats. You know what? They can. You can. All you have to do is put a good one on your head and walk outside.

The Elements of a Dress Hat

Before I get into my ideas on how to choose and wear a hat, let's start with some basics around hat materials and structure. Because dress hats are so uncommon these days, I suspect this information will be new to most people. But I think it's important to understand all the elements involved in hat construction before you start thinking about style and specifics for yourself.

FELT

Hat felt, like all the garments in this book, comes from animals. And while I proclaim the wonders and advantages of wool for knitwear and coats, it is not the best option for dress hats. It does a poor job at holding its shape and does not last very long. Rabbit felt hats are a good choice, and readily available, but the gold standard by far is beaver.

Under the coarse outer layer of a beaver's coat, there is a soft, furry coat called "beaver wool." This is what is used to create the felt that is shaped and blocked into a dress hat. Beaver is naturally warming and water resistant. In fact, if it gets wet, don't worry about it. Just re-form it into its original shape and let it air-dry. As a natural fibre, beaver is also sustainable, with a minimal environmental impact, especially if you buy a few hats and care for them, making them last a lifetime (see "Caring for Your Wardrobe").

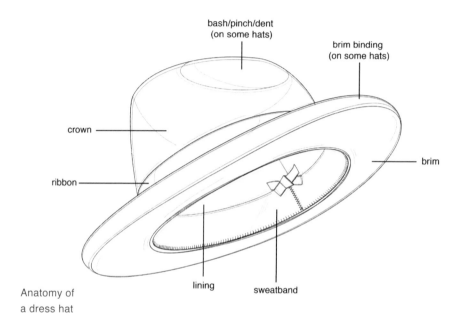

bash/pinch/dent
(on some hats)

brim binding
(on some hats)

crown

ribbon

brim

lining

sweatband

Anatomy of
a dress hat

LINING

Hat linings mostly serve an aesthetic function, but they can still be an indicator of quality. Originally, linings were used, as in other garments, to cover the unsightly stitching on the inside of hats. However, their presence today is a sign of extra care, especially if made of silk or linen, for example. It is possible, of course, for a good-quality hat to be made with no lining, but it is usually a sign of corners being cut.

HEIGHT

I don't worry too much about what all the different styles of hats are called: fedoras, trilbies, homburgs, bowlers. What I focus on are the proportions. Is the crown height (literally the height of the hat) proportionate to your head? Does it taper outward, inward, or not at all? Is the pinch deep or shallow? All of these factors can make the hat look too large or too small or simply disproportionate, even if it sits comfortably on your head.

WIDTH

Brim width is another huge factor in how a hat looks and whether it suits you. Too wide and you're entering Western hat territory — in other words, a hat that might feel costumey unless you're riding the range. But too short a brim and not only does the hat look diminutive, it also ceases to function as protection. In fact, I think the reason narrow-brimmed hats were popular a decade ago is that they almost seem to be hiding the fact they are hats, an act of self-constraint. I say don't hide. If you're going to wear a hat, wear a hat. The width of the brim needs to be in proportion to the crown, your head, and your shoulders. I don't know of a golden ratio when it comes to this proportion. It comes down to your body shape and personal preference.

COLOUR

A great piece of advice I got years ago from a trusted hat maker and friend is that your hat should contrast your jacket or overcoat, in colour or tone. That way, you look less like you're in a costume. You can never go wrong with shades of brown or grey, while dark blue can look quite dashing. As long as they are in contrast with whatever else you're wearing, of course. Consider the guide that applies to most garments: the darker, the more formal looking. That said, I have a dark-brown alpine-style hat: the casual shape trumps the formal colour.

My Hat Collection

In the entranceway of my house there are usually four or five hats hanging off the wall, a different bunch in summer and in winter. So yes, I have a lot of hats. But I like to have hats for different occasions, variable weather, and casual or formal outfits. My most formal hat is a homburg style, mid-grey hat my wife bought me a few Christmases ago. She wanted me to have something that was special, even if I didn't necessarily wear it that often. I save this hat for formal evenings, like when I wear my tuxedo, so it does feel special, indeed.

I also have a tan fedora, my first custom hat. And I've had it long enough that it's developed a patina of sorts. The pinch at the top of the crown has hardened and tarnished slightly from wear, and I love it. It doesn't look like just any hat anymore, it looks like *my* hat.

But my favourite hat, and the one I wear the most, brings together all the best qualities of a hat. It was also custom-made, so I was able to control much of the style. The crown tapers sharply inward so that it seems to follow the contours of my head. As to the shape, it's not so much pinched as bashed. The beaver felt is quite lightweight, so I am able to crunch the top of the hat in an asymmetrical way, making it look less dressy and formal, more like an out-doorsman's hat. The colour is a mid-brown that goes with pretty much everything (except my mid-brown chore coat, which is too matchy-matchy). The ribbon is thin and of the same tone as the hat, so there's little to no contrast colour-wise. Instead, the matte finish of the hat is con-trasted by the silky sheen of the ribbon. The thinness of the ribbon is meant to, once again, make the hat look more casual, but it makes the crown appear taller. And finally, the brim width is moderate, enough to give some shade but not enough to make the hat look like it belongs on a campground. But it is the overall softness of the hat I love the most. I can stuff it into my bag, scrunch it onto my head, and the rougher I am with it, the more and more its character builds. There's no other hat like it in the world, and I'm proud of that.

> If you are able to select the ribbon on a dress hat, a wide ribbon on a tall hat will make the crown look shorter and more proportionate.

Assessing Quality

Perhaps harder than assessing true quality in a hat is finding a good-quality dress hat for sale in the first place. However, a handful of good hat stores and custom hat makers are still out there. Despite the difficulty of the search, I would not recommend shopping for hats online: not only will it be hard to assess true sizing — the actual fit around your head, but also proportion, not to mention colour, are impossible to judge correctly on screen. Try hats on in person if you can find them. And then look closely at their construction.

Beaver felt is best but in itself does not guarantee quality. Poor-quality hats are more likely to have been shaped by machine. This says nothing of the hat's durability, of course, but hand shaping is usually only applied to better quality hats. Also, have a good look at the ribbon: it should look like a lovely piece of fabric, not cheap or flimsy. And as with other garments, look inside the hat. Specifically, good hats usually have high-quality sweatbands made of leather, not cloth. Leather is more comfortable and will protect the inside of the hat from, you guessed it, your sweat. Quality leather tends to be softer and more supple than cheap, stiff leather. Also, look for a lining in either silk or linen, applied with care.

In terms of construction, sweatbands and ribbons should be carefully tacked and stitched on, never glued. Glue is a cheap and easy alternative to quality construction and can't be repaired as well.

But as with other garments, a quality hat is a combination of elements working together: beaver or rabbit felt; natural-fibre lining; hand shaping and handwork; clean, even stitching; and a high-quality ribbon and sweatband. In other words, a general care and consideration for all elements in the making and styling of the hat.

Buying Your First Hat

You're not necessarily going to find all the qualities listed above when you walk into a hat shop. In fact, that is why I would recommend, if possible, that you always get your hats custommade. This gives you the best options, depending on the maker, when it comes to materials and style. However, when buying ready-made, there are some basic guidelines I can offer. Rabbit felt is a good alternative to beaver, but avoid wool. In terms of features, buying your first hat is not the time to experiment: it's about finding your style and getting used to hat wearing. So you want something you'll actually wear. Choose moderation in terms of brim width and crown height; don't go too large or too small. Try to balance them with your face shape and body type. Choose a subtle colour, again neither too light nor too dark, for versatility. And most importantly, when you're buying a hat, wear the kind of clothes that you'll wear when you own the hat.

How to Handle a Hat

A lot. Pick it up any way you like. Pinch the crown. Twist the brim. Well-made beaver felt hats are durable. Good-quality hats can take it. And in fact, they improve with age and handling. The crown may develop a unique shape based on how you put it on. Your hat may tarnish slightly, depending on where you tend to grab it. All of this gives your hat the kind of personality that can't be bought; it can only be achieved with time. So don't listen to or fret about those who treat their hats like Fabergé eggs, only picking them up gingerly by the brim and laying them softly on flat surfaces (although that is how you should treat someone *else's* hat). Throw it on your chair. Stuff it in your bag. Teach your hat who's boss.

Travelling with a Hat

One of the most difficult things about wearing a hat these days is what to do with it when it's not on your head. Because dress hats are not common, and also because many people are not used to treating clothes with care, you might be taking a risk by wearing a fine hat when going to a restaurant or travelling by plane. Okay, okay, I know, I just said you shouldn't be too precious with your hat. That is not the same, however, as having your hat stepped on and spilled on or crushed in the overhead luggage compartment. I have been travelling while hatted for a number of years and have come up with some strategies which, while not perfect, have seen me through so far.

Wearing Hats Indoors

Don't. Whether it's a restaurant, at a movie, and so on. Unless you're in a transitional space (like a foyer or train station), take your hat off. Its primary function is to protect you from the elements. Once you are out of the elements, your hat becomes purely a fashion statement. And *you* should be making your statements, not your clothes. However, there is one exception: when dining out of doors, it is acceptable to keep your hat on because it serves as a roof over your head.

RESTAURANTS

There has never been, as far as I can tell, a simple and universal solution to the problem of what to do with your hat when you sit down in a restaurant. If you are fortunate, you'll find a clothing rack or hooks nearby or the restaurant will have a coat check (long ago, some even had hat checks, but those days are gone). That said, I'd like to share a cautionary tale about leaving hats at a coat check.

I recently went out for dinner with my wife at a restaurant that also serves as a live-music venue. We left our coats at the coat check and I asked if I could leave my hat, as well. When I handed it over, the attendant tried, repeatedly, to forcibly stab the coat check ticket behind the hat ribbon (which was, of course, carefully tacked in place by hand). I quickly intervened and beseeched her to stop. I suggested instead that she just rest the ticket on the crown of the hat. She did not apologize and roughly tossed my hat onto a small shelf. Sadly, since most people do not care one squat about the welfare of their wardrobes, her behaviour was not surprising. I will say, however, that she was a rarity: in most places that have a coat check, the attendants are careful and respectful. That said, there is almost never a dedicated spot for hats, and I often worry, as I walk away with the little numbered ticket in my hand, about what dusty, dirty nook they've shoved my hat into. Sometimes the best thing to do is to simply tell the attendant, "Please handle this with care. It's a good hat."

Other options include putting your hat in your lap in a restaurant; however, this is where food spills tend to happen, so it can be risky. Never put the hat on the table because the inside of your hat is not unlike the inside of your shoe. I usually opt for an empty chair or chair back.

AIRPLANES

As plane travel became less expensive, it also became less enjoyable. Intrusive security checks, cramped spaces, and little to no patience from your fellow passengers means your belongings are in peril most of the time. That said, and as far as I know, airplanes never had special compartments to hold hats. However, because most men wore hats, airlines knew how to treat them. Today your hat is most likely to be treated by others like an old hoodie and crushed flat as they shove their oversized carry-on into the overhead compartment. I always travel with at least one hat, and I have tried a variety of solutions to ensure their safety. The best, by far, is to bring along a hat box. They are unusual and charming enough that most of the time no objections are made for the extra carry-on. They fit easily in upper compartments and pretty much ensure safe travels for your felt or straw companion. Most, if not all, good-quality hats, especially from custom makers, are sold in hat boxes.

If I travel without a box, though, this is what I do: I keep the hat on my lap until all the passengers have boarded and the overhead compartments are closed. I then search around in the compartments for a space just big enough for my hat to sit — where it hopefully won't get crushed while in transit. Crushing is not fatal, however, for a fine felt hat, which should be able to pop back into shape. A straw panama, on the other hand, might suffer permanent damage. Keep it on your lap.

The Panama Hat

A still-popular example of a technically formal hat worn casually is the panama. The classic white model, wide brimmed with a black ribbon, can be a bit of a statement, but smaller-brimmed versions in various colours seem to be gaining in popularity. The reason is simple: straw hats are more casual than felt and, therefore, don't look out of place with summer clothes. We've also grown accustomed to seeing them with a variety of outfits, from summer suits all the way to beachwear. Plus, they work: they protect your skin far better than sunblock.

While finding panama hats is easier than finding felt hats, tracking down good quality is a challenge. There are some telltale signs I look for which, again, do not guarantee quality, but point in the right direction.

I look at the weave of the hat itself — the smaller, tighter, and more even, the better, simply because it is harder to create. (A tight weave also means less breathability, so be warned.) I look for a quality ribbon and leather sweatband. In fact, a leather sweatband is much more essential in a straw hat, I've found, since when sweat dries it can quickly and irrevocably misshape the straw, shrinking it to the point of an uncomfortably tight fit. And finally, I look at the edge of the hat's brim: better made hats will have the straw turned and woven back into the brim, not cut, bent, and sewn. Again, because it is harder to do, this process is not used on cheaper hats.

Will You Wear a Hat?

A good hat enhances your wardrobe in a more impactful way than any other accessory. When worn with assurance, a good hat expresses confidence in yourself and your sense of personal style. It represents you to the world.

But I know that no matter what I say, words alone won't convince you to wear a hat if you've grown up in a world without them. And while perhaps I can make a case for why hats are practical and how you can wear them in a way that is both elegant and understated, it will take a seismic shift to bring dress hats back in popularity. But like all the other garments in this book, that's not what my argument is about.

My hope is that perhaps one guy, seeing me in a hat, will feel a little emboldened to try it himself. And to be honest, even if it's not a hat, or a sport jacket, or good leather shoes, even if it's just to put more thought into his wardrobe, to simply to dress a little better tomorrow than he did today, then my job is done.

Caring for Your Wardrobe

*I'm attached to my old clothes because I
don't have to look after them. But if clothes aren't
cared for properly when new, they
don't last to become old.*

— Stanley Ager

Clothing that's lived-in tells a story. Your story. It holds
memories, experiences, joys, and struggles. It's a reflection of who you are and how you see yourself. And the longer you
wear it, the deeper and more profound that story becomes. But it's
up to you to make sure that that story develops and unfolds.

A lot of what I write about in this book — building a quality-based sustainable wardrobe that will last for many years — is all for naught if you don't take care of what you acquire. While a pair of leather shoes can potentially last you a decade or more, that potential is in your hands. But I'll let you in on a secret that I've learned: taking care of your clothes doesn't have to feel like a chore. It can be a joy.

Spending time taking care of your clothes — polishing shoes, ironing shirts, brushing jackets — helps build a bond with your wardrobe beyond wearing it. You get to appreciate what it's made of and how it's made in a direct and tactile way. It can also be a sort of moving meditation. We know that working with our hands is good for our mental health. And so I look forward to half an hour of shirt ironing as a chance to focus on something that requires skill and attention, but is simple and repetitive. It helps to calm the mind. And those skills you develop as you learn to take better care of your clothes will help you feel better about yourself.

It all adds up to a closer relationship and bond with your clothes. You like them more, you want them to last longer, and you feel a bigger hit of joy when you put them on because of all the time and energy you've invested in them — not simply what you paid for them. They truly become yours, not just because you've worn them until they've taken on your shape (yes, this doesn't just happen to shoes; it happens to jackets, shirts, and trousers, too), but also because they've become yours as you have nurtured them, cared for them, repaired them, and given them new life when others would have thrown them away.

Caring for your garments is also a key ingredient to dressing well, in addition to a wardrobe of quality garments. On one hand, quality garments will actually look and feel better as they age if they are well taken care of. On the other hand, if an investment has been made in a garment, both emotional and financial, then that investment should be protected through ongoing care and maintenance. And since sustainability is also our goal, we can offset the impact our clothes have on the environment during production by making them last as long as possible, using a care process that requires elbow grease, not more unsustainable energy or chemicals.

Leather Shoes

When I was a kid, I never saw my father polish a pair of shoes. According to my mom it was because he didn't know how to do it properly. While in the Portuguese army, my dad had used a brush to apply black wax to his boots before polishing them to a shine. That is the army standard approach, but a brush is an imprecise tool for applying wax. Plus, my mom maintained that my dad didn't remove enough of the wax during polishing, so the bottoms of his trouser cuffs kept getting dirty.

The other reason he rarely polished is because he rarely wore leather shoes. My father was part of the generation that gave up on classic menswear except for the occasional wedding or special trip to church. Running shoes teach us very few lessons about wardrobe care.

I was, however, very familiar with the strong, slightly intoxicating smell of cheap shoe polish. It was my mother who polished shoes in our house, some of her own as well as mine and my brother's "Sunday dress" pairs. She kept an old shoebox in the basement stuffed with her supplies. When she took it down from the shelf, it was as if I were entering the workshop of an alchemist. She would lift off the worn cardboard lid to reveal ancient-looking tins, stained brushes, and soiled rags. The banged-up can of black shoe polish had me transfixed: I was attracted to its harsh smell — and still am, the same way the smell of car exhaust makes me feel nostalgic for Lisbon or Havana. But I was also frightened by the tin's power to turn almost anything it touched darker than the darkest corner of the basement.

However, like so much of my childhood, when it comes to lessons around clothing, these moments were few. We didn't own many items of quality and, therefore had little need to take care of anything. It wasn't until much, much later, when I grew up and became a father, that I started investing in my own wardrobe, especially shoes.

REGULAR MAINTENANCE

The lawn must be mowed, the garden weeded. Windows washed and stoves cleaned. Rooms need to be repainted and plumbing fixed. We take for granted that our homes need regular maintenance not only to look their best but, more importantly, to be liveable. It's sad we don't apply the same standards to our clothes, the houses we walk around in. And nothing in your wardrobe benefits more from regular maintenance than your shoes.

I'm not talking about being overly protective and precious about your footwear. Shoes are meant to get creased and a little banged up. My job, however, is to resist entropy. I like to stay aware of the state of my shoes, noticing when they might need a little TLC to bring them back to their best. On a day-to-day level, here are some things I do to keep degradation to a minimum.

Always, and I mean always, put on fine leather shoes with the help of a shoehorn. It can be made of horn, bone, wood, or steel — you can even use a credit card in a pinch — but putting shoes on without a horn will quickly and fatally damage the inside heel of your shoes. I even try to keep a tiny metal shoehorn in my day bag and for travel because, sadly, the world isn't stocked with horns the way it used to be.

Regular brushing is another habit that might, at first, seem fussy but is actually fundamental. I keep a small shoe brush by the door, and whenever I put my shoes on, before I leave the house, I give the uppers and along the seams a quick, brisk brush. Part of this is aesthetic: it helps to restore the shine of the shoe's finish. But this is also important maintenance. Removing dust and dirt is essential because they break down the leather and can wear away at the stitching in your shoes' seams.

But it turns out that the greatest threat to your shoes is not dust, dirt, or even road salt in the winter: it is your own sweat. The soles of our feet have more sweat glands per square inch than any other part of our bodies. By the end of a given day, our feet sweat as much as one

Caring for Suede Shoes

There's a common belief that suede shoes are harder to take care of than regular leather shoes. Nonsense. Since suede cannot be maintained like regular leather — with creams, conditioners and wax — you are saving yourself a lot of work. In fact, all suede shoes need is to be sprayed once a season or so with high-quality, silicone-free conditioner, which helps protect against water damage. Other than that, occasionally brushing the shoes with a suede brush, very lightly, will displace dust and dirt and restore the nap. All that said, it is true that you should avoid soaking suede shoes in a rainstorm. But despite what you might read online, you can put galoshes over suede shoes without ruining the nap of the suede. Simply cover your shoes first with an old pair of ladies' nylons.

cup of perspiration. And as that perspiration dries in our shoes, it dries out the leather and weakens seams and stitches. The heat and moisture produced by our feet isn't all bad: it helps the shoes mould to the shape of our feet. But that's while you're wearing them. When you're not, especially when you first take them off, you must put wooden shoetrees in your shoes. The wood naturally absorbs and then releases the extra moisture, adding years to the lives of your shoes.

The kinds of shoetrees you get depend, in my opinion, on the value of your shoes. The better my shoes, the better the trees. Inexpensive shoetrees still absorb moisture and help restore the shape of the shoes, but better shoetrees are made of higher-quality lighter wood and do a better job of filling up the full volume of the shoe.

And here's where I have to dispel a misunderstanding. My mother used to have a pair of heavy wooden trees that she rarely used. It turns out that she didn't understand their purpose, as many people don't. She thought they were shoe stretchers, and I can see why people may think so. Trees do actually expand your shoes a little when you put them in. But the point is to restore your shoes to their original shape and silhouette. Often, after daily wear and exposure to moisture, shoes will begin to curl up at the toes. There are two problems with that: you look like a clown (quite literally), and your shoes' creases deepen and will potentially crack when you walk and stretch the shoes out again. Shoetrees help the soles of your shoes maintain their shape while making sure creases don't get too deep in your uppers.

HOW I CARE FOR MY SHOES

I have spent a lot of time with shoemakers, cobblers, and footwear lovers and have learned invaluable lessons in shoe care from all of them. I've also learned that there is no "right" way to polish shoes. There is only your way. Shoe care is a practice and a skill that I have been developing for many years and continue to develop. I am sure, in fact, that I will go on learning, changing, and adapting as long as I live. I certainly hope that's true. That way shoe care will remain a fascinating and satisfying journey, not a dreaded chore.

The key concepts of shoe care are these: high-quality creams and polishes; cotton rags; patience; and a lot of elbow grease. Also, don't only use your eyes to judge the state of your leather but also your ears. What do I mean? Your shoes may look clean and shiny but still be in need of treatment. How can you tell? Rub the uppers with your finger: is there a rough, raspy sound, or does your finger glide over the leather almost silently? Happy leather is quiet leather. (Unless it's heavily grained leather.)

In general, I treat my shoes only about once a month unless they have suffered some calamity, like being caught in a heavy downpour. Here's what to do in that case, by the way: stuff your shoes with newspaper and let them air-dry on their sides, changing the newspaper every hour or so until the paper you remove is dry, then replace the paper with shoetrees and give the shoes a good care session. Never place the shoes near a heating element as the heat will dry the shoes out too quickly and possibly crack the leather.

CLEANING Leather dress shoes rarely need actual cleaning with soap and water because they are rarely exposed to that much dirt. That's good because soap and water dry out leather and should be used sparingly. Most often, the only cleaning your shoes need is a brisk brushing across the uppers and a small brush (like an old toothbrush) across the stitching and perhaps any broguing. You're trying to remove any accumulated dust that will eventually wear away at the leather and the seams. If your leather shoes do get properly dirty, then use a wet sponge and a leather soap — first rubbing the soap into the shoes until it lathers, then using a clean, damp sponge to remove the soap. Make sure to move on to the next step, moisturizing, as soon as the shoes are dry.

MOISTURIZING Leather is skin. The idea seems obvious, but the significance of this fact didn't sink in for me for a long time. Skin is full of natural oils that keep it healthy, vibrant, and pliant. Since shoe leather cannot naturally replenish itself, it's up to you to do the replenishing. I use a water-based conditioner that restores leather with a few applications. I use a cloth and try not to add too much on each pass, while allowing time between coats for the cream to sink in, at least fifteen minutes. This cream has no pigment so it restores only the leather's moisture. I keep adding layers until the leather doesn't soak it up any more. Give it a good buff with a shoe brush before moving on to the next step.

SHOE CREAM When my shoes are looking a bit faded or perhaps have been scuffed, I use shoe cream to not only restore colour, but also to moisturize. I apply it the same way as conditioner: with a cloth, in small amounts, letting it soak in between applications, again about fifteen minutes. One trick I learned, however, is to apply the shoe cream first, then the moisturizer. What's good about this method is that when you apply the moisturizer, it removes any excess shoe cream that might otherwise rub off on your trouser cuffs (right, Mom?).

Some quick tips for achieving a nice shine: an old, well-used shoe rag is best; use small amounts of warm water with the wax (or heat the wax by setting it on fire briefly); and finish off by buffing with an old pair of pantyhose.

POLISHING Polishing with wax serves to both protect and beautify your shoes. However, the key is to use very little (much less than you think you need), give it plenty of time to soak in (at least fifteen minutes or more), and apply numerous layers. Start with a thin layer over the entire shoe, for protection. Let it soak in, and then buff it. Then focus on applying more layers, for shine and extra protection, on the toe box and outside heel. Don't apply too much to where your shoe bends (on the instep) or the wax will build up and crack in the creases.

Shirts

Now that our shirts are mostly outerwear and on full display, they must be kept in good order. You would not wear a wrinkled and shapeless jacket, I hope, so why do that with a shirt? Especially when they are so easy to care for, in comparison to jackets. This care starts with what to do when you take your shirt off. Don't just toss it at the foot of your bed, for, as the great butler Stanley Ager said, "It's just as easy to put them away as to drop them on the

Invest in Quality Hangers

Good hangers minimize stress on a garment's fabric and help maintain shape. For shirts, use relatively thick hangers with a similar width as your shoulder, to avoid dimpling. For trousers, ensure the hanger's clamps or bars are felted, to protect the fabric from creasing or other damage. And most importantly for jackets, hangers should have large, rounded shoulders, roughly as wide as your own shoulders, to help maintain your jacket's shape. A jacket hung this way comes off the hanger in its intended three-dimensional shape, ready to wear.

floor." I differ from Mr. Ager, however, in that I don't like to store my shirts folded in a drawer. They take up a fair amount of room this way and, if left for too long, develop strong creases. And even though I use a lot of tissue paper to insure a crease-free shirt when packing luggage or performing my seasonal swap (see "How to Flip Your Seasonal Wardrobe," on page 217), it feels too fussy and time-consuming for everyday use.

Instead, I hang all my shirts. On wooden hangers. As the blog *Put This On* said so well, "Don't use wire. You're not an animal." Wire hangers dig into the shoulders and deform a shirt. Wooden hangers help the shirt maintain its shape as well as absorb a bit of moisture if the shirt has just been worn.

I like to hang my shirts back-to-back and with the top button done up, which my shirtmaker insists is unnecessary and kind of obsessive. I maintain that by hanging them back-to-back, the roll of the collar is protected, as long as your closet isn't too full. Buttoning up the top button serves two purposes: helping to ensure shirts don't slide off the hangers and — the idea my shirtmaker doesn't really believe — preserving the rounded shape of the collar lining.

I also arrange all of my shirts by colour and pattern. Obsessive, yes. Unnecessary, no. Organizing my shirts helps me overcome one of our modern ailments: decision fatigue. Your decision-making ability degrades the more decisions you have to make. I feel at ease when I open a menu at a restaurant and find only two or three items. On the other hand, the encyclopedias of food you find at most Vietnamese restaurants, for example, where the list goes well over one hundred, is nearly paralyzing. It kills conversation and can require every ounce of cognitive strength you can muster, especially at dinnertime, when you've already spent the day making decisions. And you're hungry. People in those situations tend to make poor decisions or the same one over and over (#55 Bún Thịt Nướng). And since I own a fair number of shirts, I don't want to add to that pressure. Now, instead of ten or twelve decisions, I only have two: colour or pattern.

HOW I LAUNDER MY SHIRTS

As you might expect, my advice is not "Take them to a dry cleaner." While it is easy, you are paying a cost more than money: the life of your shirts. Industrial cleaners, due to the chemicals used, harsh processes, and intense pressing, will greatly accelerate the deterioration of your shirts. Instead, why not join me in the enjoyable, cost-saving tradition of washing your shirts yourself?

Usually, you have only two places where you need to worry about dirt on a shirt: the collar and the cuffs. And that ring around the collar can be a royal pain. I have tried many, many methods, but the one I keep returning to centres around bar soap and hard work.

Start by thoroughly soaking the collar and cuffs in a bucket of clean, lukewarm water. Once the shirt is well soaked, vigorously rub in the bar soap, trying to build a lather. It turns out that the lather does a lot of the work of lifting dirt out of the shirt's fibres. Once the soap is worked in, grab the fabric and rub it against itself. I have tried toothbrushes and washboards, but nothing is as effective as the fabric itself when it comes to "ring around the collar." Rinse the collars and cuffs by continuing to rub them but this time under the water. Take them out and lather them again. But after your second rubdown, don't rinse the shirt. Bundle it up and place it, with a few other pre-treated shirts, in a plastic bag. Close up the bag and leave it for at least thirty minutes, if not overnight. The bag ensures the shirts won't dry out while the soap is performing its magic of slowly lifting out dirt.

The next morning, pull the shirts out of the bag and put them in the washing machine. I always wash my shirts in cold water on the permanent press cycle, which is rather gentle. I think this is important because washing machines, especially low water/high efficiency ones, don't do much more than get your clothes wet. You've already done most of the cleaning yourself, by hand, so this is a glorified rinse. I tend to stick to unscented, cold-water soap. I want to smell like myself — not a fake mountain breeze, thank you very much.

STAIN REMOVAL

I'm not going to provide an exhaustive list of every single type of stain you might get on your shirt and how to deal with each because, for me, stains fall into three broad categories: oily food stains, blood, and everything else.

FOOD STAINS Should tomato sauce, curry, or other oil-based food get on your clothes, you must act fast for best results. The key is to use the tools you'd used to wash greasy food off dishes: hot water and dish soap. Immediately run very hot water through the stain from the inside of the garment (hopefully pushing the offending material out). Then, using an old but clean toothbrush, apply dish soap to the spot with some vigour. Let the sudsy spot soak for up to fifteen minutes, rinse with hot water, and repeat if necessary, then launder as above. If the oily stain has dried, you can apply dish soap directly to it, without water, and rub the spot with a dry toothbrush. If this doesn't work, or if the stain is even older and drier, you must activate it — bring it back to life — in order

Cleaning Whites

I learned this one from my mother and it should be done only with white cotton garments. Before machine washing, after you have thoroughly sudsed up the stained areas of the garment with soap and water, lay the clothes out in the sunshine for a few hours, periodically rewetting them if the sun dries the fabric. The sun will naturally bleach out the stains.

to get the oil out. Counterintuitively, what I've found works best is WD-40. I spray a tiny amount on the affected spot and immediately cover it in baking soda. Next I allow it to sit for up to an hour, then vacuum off the soda. The soda helps to draw out some of the oil and the WD-40. I then use the previously outlined hot water/dish soap method to remove the rest of the oil.

BLOOD Blood is a relatively easy stain to remove, in my experience. But once again, speed is of the essence. If the stain is relatively new, simply soak the garment in cold water for a few hours. Most of the time, the stain will disappear on its own. If there is any left, I use the hand-cleaning method described earlier for cuffs and collars before machine washing. If the blood stain has set, try soaking the garment in cold salted water for a few hours. Another option is to try dish soap, as above, but in cold water rather than hot. Heat will set the stain in the fabric.

GENERAL STAINS Most other stains, I find, can be treated with the previously described hand-cleaning method (lather, cold water, fabric on fabric rubbing). It may take more time, more soaking, but usually it works. In all cases, make sure you get the stain out before you apply any heat to your shirt (dryer or iron) as heat will set the stain almost permanently in the cloth.

DRYING

I always hang-dry my shirts, never tumble dry. Again, the heat of the dryer can set stains and I fear the strain of tumbling around in there does more damage than good. Not to mention the unnecessary use of energy — this is a chance to offset the environmental impact your shirts had during production. Let your shirts air-dry while you contemplate the best part of cleaning your own shirts: pressing.

HOW I PRESS A SHIRT

A couple of years ago a video of a man pressing a shirt went viral. It starts with a big, wide table, a small man, a white shirt, and an iron. The video is almost fetishistic. The man quickly but methodically lays out the shirt and irons it in a way I'd never seen before. He starts with the front plackets. Then the sleeves. Then the collar. Then he

Formaldehyde

In case you think you've discovered a magic workaround to this "ironing a shirt" thing, thanks to non-iron shirts, I have one word for you: formaldehyde. The fabric for non-iron shirts is treated with a chemical, dimethyloldihydroxyethyleneurea, and heated, causing changes at the molecular level that make the fabric crease resistant. A by-product of the chemical process is formaldehyde, a known carcinogen. Little to none of it ever comes into contact with you, but if you are concerned, even a little, with the environment, is it really a worthwhile trade-off to put more chemicals in the world, deadly chemicals, just to save you thirty minutes of work every couple of weeks?

lays the shirt flat and irons the inside of the back. Then he buttons some of the shirt buttons and irons the front. Finally, he turns the shirt over and masterfully folds it into a perfect display model.

I think most people watched the video to see a pro at work and marvel at his technique. There is also something mesmerizing and even meditative about his process. But I studied the video like the proverbial student learning from a master. I took in every movement and every technique. I, too, wanted to iron a shirt perfectly. But I didn't have the right tools, which would stop most people long before they even thought to themselves "I'm going to get into ironing shirts." The first thing I needed was an ironing table.

I hate ironing boards. They are awkward and tippy and I don't know how many times my old home iron has slipped, fallen off, and crashed to the ground. It has the battle scars to show for it. So even though I wanted to properly take care of my clothes and iron my own shirts, I hated the process. Maybe a proper table would change all that? I found a Martha Stewart how-to on making an ironing table on YouTube. It required a trip to a hardware store for a sheet of plywood. Then a trip to a fabric store for some sheets of heavy cloth and muslin, fabric glue, and tape. And I borrowed a powerful staple gun from a friend.

The work was pretty straightforward, folding sheet after sheet over the board, carefully and methodically stapling each into place *just so*. The final step was to apply fabric tape that not only made sure everything was sealed and wouldn't come undone, but ensured the table met the Martha standard of craftsmanship and obsessiveness. There isn't a loose bit of fabric anywhere, and after years of use it still has a lovely, firm bounce to its surface. I am very proud of my table and often bring guests to my basement to show it off.

So there I was, the table finally built and set up, iron nice and hot and steamy. And a washed but wrinkled shirt. As sheer a pleasure it was to have the vast expanse of the table to work on, it took me many, many shirts to unlearn how I had learned to iron. This new table technique I've discovered is not instinctual. Ironing the inside of the shirt seemed wrong. And it sometimes felt like I wasn't getting every nook and cranny.

But over time, my technique got better, I developed my own style, and now I actually look forward to ironing. Yes, I look forward to ironing. I turn on some music or a podcast and I have a thirty-minute moving meditation that not only calms my mind but means I have a closet full of beautifully pressed shirts.

PRESSING A SHIRT, STEP BY STEP Here is how I press a shirt. And by the way, *press* is the key word because, like the gentleman in the video shows us, a fair amount of pressure goes a long way in getting rid of stubborn wrinkles. Plus, you're mostly pressing down, not just moving back and forth.

The key to a good press is moisture and heat. Moisture relaxes the fabric while heat stiffens it again. Considering your newly laundered shirts will be covered with wrinkles, you need to dampen them before pressing. I use a spray bottle of clean water and lightly coat the area I'm about to press. Then, when you apply the iron, you get a satisfying sizzle and a sharp, smooth finish. I use steam from the iron rarely instead of reaching for the spray bottle, only on stubborn spots as I'm working away. And while it is by no means the only way to do it, this is my ironing process.

1. Press the front plackets.
2. Press the collar but never where the collar meets the collar band. If there is a bit of a ring there, ironing it will make it permanent. Avoid the collar tips as ironing there can burn the fabric, producing shininess.

3. Iron the sleeves: first, the cuffs, on the inside; second, the sleeves themselves. Don't iron right to the edge of the sleeve or you'll get a strong crease.
4. Lay the shirt open on the table. Iron the back of the shirt from the inside.
5. Button up the collar and a button halfway down the placket so that the shirt stays in place. Lay the shirt down as smoothly as possible and iron each side of the front of the shirt.
6. Slip a wooden hanger into position and hang the shirt, ready to wear.

Sport/Suit Jackets

I used to think there was something magical or mystical to explain why jackets are dry clean only. What, exactly, would happen if they got wet? Would all the colour run? Would the fabric dissolve? It turns out the explanation involves neither magic nor mysticism. There are two reasons jacket should never be washed like other garments. The first is structure: jackets are constructed with layers of cloth and many stitches to have a three-dimensional shape around your chest. The standard washing and pressing process would destroy this shape. The second issue is fabric: worsted and other types of wool used in jackets are prone to shrinkage and other ill effects if washed in water. But here's the good news: jackets rarely need to be cleaned.

Unless you have stained your jacket, most dirt can simply be brushed off. In fact, brushing your suit is something that should

The Clothes Brush

My mom tells me that when she was growing up, a clothes brush was always close at hand. And certainly not because she had a lady's maid. In fact, it was the opposite. My mother grew up in a tiny village in near poverty, and caring for clothes was an issue of survival. Her family knew that occasionally brushing clothes, almost all clothes, was an effective deterrent to the damage that dirt and stains can do. I love my double-sided natural-bristle brush: one side for suits, jackets, and trousers, the other side for sweaters. It's even effective at getting mud off my jeans: I just wait until the mud dries then brush it off completely. The result is less laundering, which saves time, energy, and money.

be done either before or after each time you wear it. Acquire a good-quality clothes brush and always brush in long vertical strokes. I tend to first stroke up toward the shoulders, then down. Never brush back and forth like a toothbrush, but do get into every nook and cranny: behind the lapel, under the arms, even under pocket flaps. These are places where dirt and small specks of dried food can lodge and cause bigger problems in the future.

If a more sizable stain has dried, I do something I've seen many a tailor do: scrape at it with your fingernail. This simple trick can be amazingly effective. Tightly woven worsted wool is relatively impervious to larger elements, so bigger bits can be removed with gentle scraping.

If, however, you have a serious food stain or an accumulation of dirt from a lot of wear, then your jacket or suit needs to be dry cleaned. I keep dry cleaning to a minimum because I know what's involved, and it isn't the best for your garment. First of all, the "dry" part refers only to the fact that no water is used in the cleaning process. Instead, your jackets and suits are loaded into industrial washing machines and washed in a chemical solvent called Perchloroethylene or "perc" for short. The chemical itself isn't so much a problem for the fabric (except it does mean more chemicals in the world), but it's how the solvent is used. To save money, some cleaners reuse the solvent more than it should be, which means leaving more dirt in your clothes.

My other concern with dry cleaning jackets and suits is the pressing. As I wrote, a jacket is crafted to have a shape. Part of that shape is achieved by construction, but much of it is accomplished by pressing. It used to be that tailors would do something called a "sponge and press," where they would press a jacket back into shape. Almost no one does this anymore. And most dry cleaners don't know how to press shape back into a jacket after it has been washed. Those who do charge a fair bit of money, which makes sense. Hand-pressing a suit is skill intensive and time-consuming.

And so, I dry clean very rarely. I find most of my jackets can go a year between cleaning, and suits, which I wear more rarely, even two years. The biggest reason I dry clean them at all is the prevention of clothing moths and the seasonal swap, which we'll discuss in a moment.

Trousers

While most wool trousers should be dry cleaned, most cotton and linen trousers can be washed and pressed in a manner similar to shirts. For instance, on light-coloured trousers I pre-treat the cuffs as I do with shirts. However, there are some differences. I tend to press my trousers inside out because sometimes, with all the folds and creases, the heat of an iron passing over trousers can burn the fabric, leaving it shiny. Also, the waist is a tricky area to press and requires extra time and attention, or even specialized tools like tailoring hams and sleeve boards.

Pressing a crease into the fronts of trouser legs is also a tricky business but very satisfying. Here's how I do it: with the trousers flipped right side out, line up the cuffs so that the seams are on top of each other. Lay the trousers on their side and try to keep the seams on top of each other, running all the way up to the crotch. If there are pleats on your trousers, make sure that the crease you're creating in the front meets up perfectly with the pleat. In fact, use the pleat as your guide: begin pressing from pleat down the trouser leg. When this front crease is done, you'll notice that the backs of the trousers are wavy and not smooth. That is because shape is built into the legs; the front and back are shaped differently from each other (or should be, on well-tailored garments). Pull the backs of the legs lengthwise until the back crease is smooth and press it sharp. Be extra mindful around the knees where the fabric may be stretched out a bit. You want to restore it as much as possible to its original shape. Flip the trousers over and repeat these steps on the other leg. Hang the trousers either from the cuffs in a clamp or folded over a felted trouser hanger.

Knitwear

I tend to wash my sweaters rarely because of the work involved. Plus, since sweaters don't sit next to your skin, they don't tend to get too dirty. While a fair amount of work, washing does more than freshen up your knitwear. A buildup of dirt can lead to friction, which will break down fibres. Which leads to the dreaded pill. Washing will help reduce pilling somewhat, but pilling is inevitable and not a sign that your sweater is poor quality. It is simply a reality of wool.

Many quality sweaters should be dry cleaned, as per their labels, but many do well with a handwash. This is a simple process that you should do with one sweater at a time. Start by putting wool-washing soap or baby shampoo into a basin (gentle soap is the key), then add water that is neither cold nor hot: on the cooler side of lukewarm. Soak the sweater for a few minutes. Then gently push the soapy water through the sweater a few times, never wringing. Empty the basin and refill with fresh

Dealing with Pilling

When pilling gets bad, I use a fabric shaver. Because you are actually applying blades to your clothing, you must be very careful and deliberate, as if you were shaving your face with a straight razor. That said, I have yet to cause any damage to my sweaters. To use a fabric shaver, first, lay out the sweater on a flat, firm surface. Make sure the knitwear is stretched out slightly. Then run the shaver over the pilling area lightly and gingerly.

Another less hazardous method is to use an emery board and lightly stroke the affected area until the pilling is removed. Do not scrub, but rather, stroke in one direction.

water, gently kneading the sweater until no more bubbles appear in the water. This may take three or four basins of fresh water. Once all the soap is gone, squeeze out as much water as you can, but never wring or twist the sweater.

You then have two options for removing most of the water from your sweater. The quicker method is to place your sweater in a sealed mesh bag or pillowcase and run it through the spin cycle of your washing machine. Sealing the sweater in ensures it doesn't stretch while the spin cycle gets most of the water out. The other option is to roll up the wet sweater in a dry, clean towel and press down hard.

Next, lay the sweater out on a clean towel to dry completely. You can, at this point, lightly pull and press the sweater into shape with your hands. Make sure no part of the sweater hangs down or experiences the pull of gravity, which can stretch it out of shape. A sweater can take a day or more to dry, depending on the humidity of your drying room and how much water you were able to remove before laying it out. Make sure your knitwear is bone dry before putting it away.

Some of my thinner merino sweaters end up wrinkly after washing. I turn them inside out and, with either an iron guard or a thin sheet of cotton between the iron and sweater, I press (not iron) repeatedly and lightly, using steam to get out the wrinkles.

When it comes to heavy, chunky sweaters, I would dry clean them because of the possibility of them getting stretched out with the weight of all that water.

And once your knitwear is clean, storage also helps maintain it for the future. Fold your sweaters carefully and don't stuff your drawers with them. The friction of opening and closing a too-full drawer will damage the fibres and cause pilling.

Overcoats

Similar to jackets and suits, overcoats usually have shape built into them and should not be washed in water. Occasional brushing is all they need, with a dry clean every few years or so.

Socks

Washing machines do not eat socks. And socks don't disappear into some kind of laundry room Bermuda triangle. Socks just have a tendency to get stuck in the nooks and crannies of your machine or fall behind the furniture. But trust me — once you start spending more on your socks, as you should, you will work much harder to keep track of them and care for them properly.

Thankfully, sock laundering is straightforward: wash them in cold water and hang them to dry. I never machine dry as the heat tends to negatively affect elasticity and can shrink wool socks. Left hanging overnight, socks are usually dry by the next day with little effort (except for the seemingly endless process of hanging each individually). Socks do tend to look rumpled and out of shape after hanging to dry, but if you slightly stretch them out flat, they will return to near normal shape.

HOW I STORE MY SOCKS

Figuring out a system for storing your socks can be as daunting as solving the puzzle of how a farmer can cross a river in a small boat with a fox, a chicken, and a bag of grain. You want your socks to be organized and paired up, but you don't want to stretch them in any way. Or have them eat each other. Thankfully, after giving it much thought and trying various methods — and I'm not talking about the river thing, good luck with that — I've found a way, and it's not what I used to do. Once upon a time, I would either fold one sock opening over its twin, which stretched the sock needlessly, or fold them in half over each other, which meant they could get separated and my sock drawer was the site of a daily fishing expedition.

Here's what I do now: lay one sock out as flat as it will go. Lay the other sock symmetrically on top of it. Starting at the toes, roll the socks up together tightly. The roll and the fabric itself should keep the socks in a stable bundle, which you can arrange in rows in your sock drawer. Happy socks, easy to find.

HOW I REPAIR MY SOCKS

Despite buying really good socks and then washing, drying, and storing them carefully, you will eventually feel the disappointment of a small hole. Mine always appear under my heels. I'll take my shoes off and when my foot lifts off the floor there's that brief moment when my heart breaks a little: I feel a spot of cold on my foot or my skin sticks slightly to the floor. But a small hole is not the end of your beautiful socks. That is, not if you act fast. It's time to darn.

The wonderful thing about darning socks is that it's one of the easiest repairs you can make to your wardrobe but it has the biggest impact. A few minutes of sewing saves a garment from the landfill. For a little while, at least. And it doesn't even matter how good or bad your sewing technique is because no one will see the patch job. Here's my simple darning technique, step by step:

1. Place a round or egg-shaped object in the sock and secure it under the hole with an elastic band. I use a small, expired halogen light bulb because it produces a nice, flat surface to work on.

2. Using a sewing needle (a regular one is fine if you don't have a darning needle), choose a thread as close to the colour of the socks as possible.

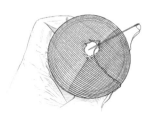

3. Start by sewing around the edges of the hole to help reinforce the fabric.

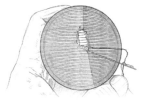

4. Sew across the hole in one direction using simple in/out stitches, pulling only slightly (but not enough to close the hole yet).

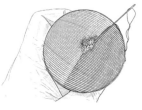

5. Sew across the hole perpendicular to your first set of stitches, threading through those stitches as much as you can.

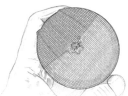

6. Tie off the ends and snip the excess thread.

Leather Gloves

Leather gloves, like shoes, need care and maintenance for the leather to age well. However, the process is not as involved or intense as shoes. In fact, it requires only one step: moisturizing. Usually once a season, with any leather gloves that don't have a suede-like finish, I use garment-specific cream. Creams might make the leather slightly darker, so consider trying it on the bottom of the glove first if you're not sure you'll like the results. Here's what I do: I put one of the gloves on and with fabric wrapped around the fingers of my other hand (as with shoe polishing), I rub a small amount of cream all over the glove. I repeat this on my other glove, which requires some ambidextrous moisturizing, and let the gloves sit for at least fifteen minutes. I then use a clean cloth to rub off any residual cream, a step that also serves to slightly polish the gloves.

Now, one advantage to black gloves, of course, is that they don't really show dirt. Once you start wearing brown gloves, especially lighter brown or other colours, you'll start noticing the dirt. If the dirt starts to really tarnish your gloves, you can wash them in water (after you've checked with the maker's instructions).

Washing gloves is also relatively straightforward: essentially you will wash your hands while wearing the gloves. After putting the gloves on, dampen them with cool water. Then take a bit of leather soap and work up a lather all over the gloves. Take the gloves off and rinse them thoroughly in cool water, then squeeze out any excess water (never wring them). Roll the gloves in a clean towel to get rid of any extra water, kneading for a couple of minutes but, again, never wringing. Blow air into gloves to restore a bit of shape. And before the gloves fully dry, put them on to restore more of their shape. Washing leather does dry it out so it is essential that you moisturize your gloves at this point, as previously described.

Dress Hats

Hat maintenance is, thankfully, a relatively easy task. Chances are that unless you seriously soil your hat, all it will require is the occasional brushing to remove excess dust and restore the nap. To do this, hold the hat in your non-dominant hand with your fingers spread out to stabilize it. Then, using a natural-bristle clothes brush, turn the hat either counter-clockwise or clockwise, brushing in the opposite direction. The direction you brush will be based on the nap of your hat's felt: always brush with the nap.

The first time one of my custom-made beaver felt hats got seriously wet in the rain, my wife panicked, thinking it was ruined. But it's beaver — it's made to get wet. I simply let it hang-dry, after gently encouraging it toward its intended shape, and it was as good as new.

Should your hat require more substantial assistance, like stain removal, re-blocking, or repair, then you will have to find a hat service, which is sadly getting harder and harder to locate.

HOW I STORE MY HATS

As I have said, don't be too precious with your hats. I know, because I've been down that road. After I bought my first custom fedora, I handled it gingerly and only by the brim. I hung my hat ever so carefully each time I took it off. And I never put any pressure on the crown in an effort to maintain its shape. But no matter my care and diligence, the brim started to bend and the crown to soften. And that's okay. In fact, it's what you want. All those great hats you see in old movies? Those hats so full of character and personality? They weren't made that way. They achieved their misshapen glory because they were worn, beaten up, and lived in. I'm not suggesting you intentionally sit on or distress your hat. However, feel free to grab it by the dimple or crown and throw it onto a chair when you get home. (Never pick up someone else's hat by the crown, however, only the brim — their personality is not your responsibility.) Sure, invest in a proper hat rack for day-to-day storage, but when you are out and about wearing the hat, live in it; don't carry it around like a baby bird in a nest of spun sugar.

For long-term storage, over the winter or summer, I keep my hats in their original hat boxes in my closet. This way, they are protected from needless dust and damage while maintaining their shape. Stuff your hats with tissue paper to give them a bit of help. I realize I just went on and on about not being too precious with your hats, but improper long-term storage can actually cause problems like creases in the nap, not build character.

How to Flip Your Seasonal Wardrobe

My mom used to tell me stories about how obsessive my grand-mother was about spring cleaning. The oven would be pulled away from the wall so my mom could get back there to clean. All the furniture was moved out of room after room so my mom could clean thoroughly. Every piece of china and cutlery was removed from the kitchen so it could all be rewashed and dusted. By my mom. At the time it just seemed like my mom was endlessly clean-ing while my grandmother did … what? Delegated? I realize now the impact those stories had on me: I have an almost religious need to clean in spring. If I don't, unseen filth will grow and accumulate in the dark recesses of my home until eventually my family and I are swallowed up and never seen again.

That said, I don't do an old-school Portuguese cleaning of my house every spring. Mostly. However, I do apply that obsessive attention to my wardrobe with a seasonal flip. And while I know it's good for my clothes, it also keeps my obsessive cleaning de-mons at bay.

The seasonal wardrobe flip is also one reason I don't get tired of dressing with intent: twice a year I pack up all my clothes and get a whole new batch. I'm not throwing away the old and buying new — as many people do today — but storing one set of clothes while unpacking another. This is an old idea and one most often practised by women. As more and more men return to building sustainable wardrobes, however, the potentially higher quality and more diverse clothing comes with a need for special care. Combine that with limited closet space, and it becomes necessary to store away the clothes you don't use for long periods of time.

I'll warn you straight away that this involves a fair amount of work. There's cleaning, sorting, repairing, travelling to and from the dry cleaner, packing, and unpacking. But the advantages far outweigh the work: your clothes will last longer if properly taken care of; you get to rediscover some of your favourite items; the switch of seasons becomes even more marked and special; and you get a new wardrobe without spending any money.

This is a key point and a strategy I've found to get over the dopamine hit of buying new clothes. If during the winter, for example, my summer clothes are put away and out of sight, I forget about them. Instead of seeing my linen shirts and cotton shorts in my cupboards every day, even as I reach for sweaters and cords, I'm hardly aware that summer exists. Then in the spring, when I make the switch, it's as if I've bought a whole new set of clothes. Without the spending or environmental impact, but with a similar emotional hit of joy.

PURGE AND REPAIR

A great advantage to doing a seasonal swap is that you get the chance to have a good look at your wardrobe. This is often the time when I realize I have an item I haven't worn all season and it's time to find it a new home. Also, this is when I finally get around to fixing a loose button, darning a sock, or making any other small repair I may not have noticed during the season.

The Dreaded Clothes Moth

One reason to do a seasonal swap carefully and meticulously, as many have learned only too late, is to avoid the clothes moth. Any tiny specks of food, dirt, or even sweat left on your clothes are breeding grounds for moth eggs that, when they hatch, release hungry, hungry larvae who will eat up your precious suits and sweaters. So do everything you can to get your clothes as clean as possible, then make sure you store them properly. Storing garments bone dry in plastic bins, off the ground, with ventilation holes drilled in the tops of the bins has worked for me for years.

DRY CLEANING

Despite having a dry cleaner I trust, I don't dry clean that often. It can get expensive, and if the suit isn't worn much or doesn't have a smell or stain or mark I can remove myself, I don't dry clean. But when it comes to the seasonal swap, I assess all my suits for cleanliness. This keeps the dry cleaning down to perhaps once or twice a year for most of my suits and jackets. That said, dry cleaning is the best way to get rid of moth eggs; although, moths will still happily lay new eggs once your suit is in storage.

STEAMING

Suits and jackets that aren't dry cleaned cannot be machine or handwashed. Instead, I do a combination of brushing and steaming. The heat of the steamer will, of course, remove creases and wrinkles. I like to think it will also kill any moth eggs I happen to catch, so I give my pants and vests a good steaming. With suit jackets, I steam only the arms and back because the steam will re-shape or even damage the structure in the front, lapels, and collar.

BRUSHING

I've discussed brushing clothing on a regular basis, but this is especially important in a seasonal swap. Not only will this hopefully dislodge any moth eggs in the fabric, but it will also remove specks of dust and dirt. Friction caused by moving in your clothes can break down the fibres if little bits of dust and dirt are present. With long strokes, start by brushing from the bottom up, then from the top down.

CLEANING

Every garment should be as clean and dry as possible before being stored. Follow all the cleaning procedures outlined previously. Because of the threat of moths, knitwear is especially worth a careful cleaning. Sweaters should be washed — either dry cleaned or handwashed — before long-term storage.

Packing Clothes in Tissue Paper

Inside my large plastic containers, all my clothes are packed carefully with tissue paper. This helps negate the effects of any condensation that may occur. This also ensures the clothes, especially shirts and pants, do not develop deep creases. It is a great pleasure, every six months, to open a container and find that my clothes are ready to wear, without a pressing.

STORAGE

In an ideal world, I would have a huge cedar closet in my basement for all my seasonal clothes-storage needs. Right next to that would be my walk-in humidor along with a full wine cellar. Until that day comes, I have to settle for plastic. For my sweaters, casual pants, socks, and other small items, I use large plastic storage containers. Make sure bins are stored off the floor on a shelf so that bugs can't crawl in. To make sure your clothes don't get mouldy, drill holes in the top of the container. I know these seem like perfect little doorways for bugs, but since clothes are packed as clean as possible, it's more important to let humidity escape as the plastic is not at all breathable.

GARMENT BAGS

The clear choice for packing suits and jackets is garment bags, which keep clothing dust-free and form at least some barrier against moths. I never use bags fully made of plastic, however, as they do not breathe, and any moisture that might be left in your suit or jacket will cause mould or a nasty smell in a plastic bag.

STORING SHOES

Every pair of my shoes or boots gets one more cleaning, moisturizing, and polishing before they are put away for the season. But unlike during regular maintenance, this time I'm also looking for any serious issues or damage that may have to be dealt with. I ensure that shoe trees are in place, and then every pair is placed inside shoe bags for the season.

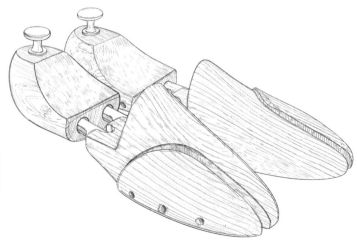

The preferred shape and design for wooden shoe trees

Shoe bags are soft cotton bags, just a bit bigger than a shoe, with a drawstring closure. Each shoe should be in its own bag, not doubled up lest they scuff each other. I once asked a lifelong butler if it was necessary to first wrap the shoes in tissue paper as they do on *Downton Abbey*, and he looked at me like I was mad. Once properly packed inside their bags, my shoes are placed carefully in the closet (not thrown or piled) to await their season, ready to be worn the moment they emerge.

Getting Dressed

The sense of being perfectly well-dressed
gives a feeling of tranquility that
religion is powerless to bestow.
— Ralph Waldo Emerson

It sounds a bit silly because, of course, by the age of six or seven most of us know how to dress ourselves. But I'm not talking about just pulling on a pair of trousers and a shirt. Once you decide to dress with intention, you realize it can involve a fair amount of planning and preparation. And if there is something I love, something I look forward to and relish, it is planning and preparation. I have been known to book a family vacation eight months in advance, with every day's events scheduled and set up. But that doesn't mean I'm not spontaneous. After all, when is spontaneity more enjoyable than when it happens in the midst of precise planning and preparation?

So yes, I am unabashedly detail-oriented. Some might even say obsessive. It must be why I feel such kinship and draw so much inspiration from the valets and butlers of old. It was their charge and responsibility to make sure everything was in order, just so, put right, shipshape, as it should be. To indulge in some pop psychology, I guess it's how I try to keep my own deep-seated demons of disorder at bay. But this is a book about getting dressed, not getting depressed, so let's move on.

One of the main duties of the valet is to dress their gentleman. This usually begins well in advance of the actual getting dressed bit. The valet considers the day's activities and picks out an ensemble they think is most appropriate and that their employer would most enjoy wearing. They then set about getting all the pieces ready. In this day and age (and yes, there are still valets in this day and age), they almost never actually dress their gentleman. Without the clumsy and difficult rigours of detached collars and two-sided cufflinks, most employers can dress themselves. However, the job of the contemporary valet is to have the entire outfit not just picked out but laid out in such a way as to make dressing fast and efficient. For instance, using a clothes stand (also called a butler or valet stand), the shirt, jacket, and pants are hung and easily accessible. The belt or suspenders are already attached to the pants. The socks are picked out and partially folded inside out, so the employer can simply slip his feet in and pull them up. And a shoehorn is conveniently laid across the shoes.

There is no need for these extremes, of course, if you are laying out clothes for yourself. But laying out your own clothes can offer the best of both worlds: the skill and care of a valet and the joy of building your own outfit, not someone else's. You get to choose exactly how you want to face the day, how to put all the pieces together, how to present yourself. A big part of dressing well should be the joy of it. I take pleasure from my clothes and picking them out is as much fun as it is creative and expressive. However enjoyable it is, though, I strongly suggest doing this choosing the night before.

Traditional valet/butler stand

The excuse I hear from a lot of guys as to why they don't wear classic garments is that they don't have the time and energy first thing in the morning to pick out an outfit. As if their closets are full of impeccably tasteful and elegant clothes, but in their rush to get to work, they just happen to pick the T-shirt and jeans lying on the floor at the foot of their bed. Of course, first you need an excellent wardrobe. But once you are on your way sartorially, I will agree that the morning is not always the best time to be spoiled for choice. You may be late for an appointment or in a sleepy daze. You don't want to get to your morning meeting only to realize your tie and pocket square are exactly the same colour or pattern, like those of the head waiter of an upscale pub. Plus, you will face a lot of decisions during your day, each of them wearing you down just a little bit. As fun as it is to pick an outfit, you don't want to exhaust that decision-making reservoir so early in the day.

Instead, take a few minutes before bed to prepare your next day's outfit. Think of it as a mind-cleansing, day-ending ritual. It's also something that can lead to a better night's sleep because you know at least one thing is in place for tomorrow. I usually start with whatever jacket or suit I want to wear, as that will have the biggest overall impact on the outfit. Then I place whatever shirt I think works best on the valet stand and drape the jacket over top. At this point, I can start experimenting with ties if I'm going to wear one. The valet stand acts as a sort of mannequin. And I shouldn't have to say this, but don't pre-tie your tie; you're not seven years old. The tie will be forever creased and you won't be able to lengthen or shorten the blade to go with the rise of your pants. Instead, I drape my tie over an end of my stand. Once I have the tie settled, I can choose the pocket square. I don't usually leave the square in the pocket the night before; in my opinion, the way you fold or puff the square is dependent on your mood. There's no telling at night how serious or flamboyant I'm going to feel tomorrow.

I don't thread my belts on to my pants in advance, mostly because I rarely wear belts. I find them uncomfortable and they do a relatively bad job at the one thing they are supposed to: hold up your pants. Instead, with most of my trousers I use suspenders. These I do attach to my pants the night before. I once saw a guy — in an online video, not by peeking through his window — attach his suspenders after he put his pants on, but he's an Italian style icon and I leave that kind of thing to the professionals.

Lastly, I usually pick out hosiery and underwear in the morning because they require less thought and preparation. In fact, socks fall into that pocket square folding category: an opportunity for spontaneity in an otherwise fully planned outfit.

This is the way I get dressed and hopefully it can inspire you and give you permission to think more deeply about your clothes. Regardless of how you do it, what should primarily drive you when getting dressed is not decorum or occasion or the expectations of others, but joy. The joy of great clothing, clothing that is well made, of excellent materials, that fits you well. The joy of combining that clothing in a way only you can. And perhaps that is the key to overcoming the dopamine-fed rush of buying new, disposable clothing: nurturing the deeper, more satisfying joy of owning, caring for, and wearing good clothes.

ACKNOWLEDGEMENTS

In many ways, I've been working on this book for a decade and a half, since I first started rethinking my wardrobe. Which means my wife, Marijke, has been subjected to an ungodly amount of talk about lapel widths and shoe styles. I have to thank her, with all my heart, for her patience and encouragement as I went through a process of self-discovery. I thank her especially for the time I spent making this book, months of evenings and weekends spent researching and writing instead of cleaning the house and walking the dog.

Though my dad never had a tailor to take me to, he did show me how to tie a tie. In fact, he first taught me when I was in grade six, for a tie-tying competition at my school. I came in first. Well, I *tied* for first. Never properly thanked you for that, Papa. It was my mom who taught me the joy of caring for my clothing (and my home). I am thankful I got to see her shine shoes and iron clothes and to hear stories of how they used to do it all when she was a little girl in a tiny Portuguese village.

No one had a greater impact on this book's spirit than G. Bruce Boyer. Bruce has not only been my greatest influence when it comes to dressing, but he also inspired me to write with more passion and personal expression. Along those lines, I have to thank Daemon Fairless for reminding me to bring joy and sensuality into my writing. And my dear friend Stephen Temkin for giving me the kick in the backside I needed to stop apologizing for my sense of style and, instead, to celebrate it.

I want to thank the folks at Dundurn, especially publisher Scott Fraser for his excitement when I first shared the idea with him, and associate publisher Kathryn Lane for her support during the pandemically challenged process. Special thanks to editor Kate Unrau, who, like a fine tailor, took my original words and applied such skillful alterations; she transformed the prose into something far better than I could have hoped. And to Firdaus Ahmed for bringing the book to life with his astonishingly detailed and lyrical illustrations.

None of it could have happened, though, without the tireless work of my literary agent and friend, Philip Turner, who believed in the idea so strongly from the start that he wouldn't rest until he saw it in print. My sincere thanks, Philip.

And there are also a group of craftspeople, makers, sellers, writers, and menswear gurus who have been invaluable in offering me advice, guidance, and the push in the right direction: Massimiliano Bresciani, Audie Charles, Perry Ercolino, Richard Sebastian Espinosa, Emanuel Farré, Peter Feeney, Zach Jobe, Vincent Metzger, Bernhard Roetzel, Jean-Baptiste Rosseeuw, Anda Rowland, Gary Tok, and last but certainly not least, Bo Yang. I thank you all so much for your time, insights and encouragement.

BIBLIOGRAPHY

Ager, Stanley, and Fiona St. Aubyn. *The Butler's Guide to Running the Home and Other Graces*. New York: Clarkson Potter, 2012.

Antongiovanni, Nicholas. *The Suit: A Machiavellian Approach to Men's Style*. New York: HarperCollins, 2006.

Boyer, G. Bruce. *Elegance: A Guide to Quality in Menswear*. New York: W. W. Norton, 1987.

———. *Eminently Suitable*. New York: W. W. Norton, 1990.

———. *True Style*. New York: Basic Books, 2015.

Breward, Christopher. *The Suit*. London: Reaktion Books, 2016.

Flusser, Alan. *Dressing the Man*. New York: HarperCollins, 2002.

———. *Style and the Man*. New York: HarperCollins, 2010.

Hand, Douglas. *The Laws of Style: Sartorial Excellence for the Professional Gentleman*. Chicago: American Bar Association, 2018.

MacPherson, Charles. *The Butler Speaks*. Toronto: Appetite by Random House, 2013.

Mair, Carolyn. *The Psychology of Fashion*. New York: Routledge, 2018.

O'Brien, Glenn. *How to Be a Man: A Guide to Style and Behavior for the Modern Gentleman*. New York: Rizzoli International Publications, 2011.

Raef, Malie. *Dress Shirt Design*. New York: Schiffer, 2007.

Roetzel, Bernard. *Gentleman: A Timeless Guide to Fashion*. Potsdam, Germany: h.f.ullmann, 2015.

———. *A Guy's Guide to Style*. Potsdam, Germany: h.f.ullmann, 2012.

Schoeffler, O.E., and William Gale. *Esquire Encyclopedia of 20th Century Men's Fashions*. New York: McGraw-Hill, 1973.

Sitwell, Constance. *Complete Home Care of Your Family Wardrobe*. New York: Arco, 1944.

Smith, Russell. *Men's Style: The Thinking Man's Guide to Dress*. Toronto: McClelland & Stewart, 2005.

Villarosa, Ricardo, and Giuliano Agneli. *Homo Elegans*. Milan: Idealibri S.R.L., 1992.

Windsor, Edward (Duke of). *Windsor Revisited*. Boston: Houghton Mifflin, 1960.

ABOUT THE AUTHOR

Pedro Mendes is the co-author of *Walter Beauchamp: A Tailored History of Toronto*, a book about Canada's oldest custom tailor. He is regularly heard on CBC Radio, writing and hosting documentaries about men's style, masculinity, and the fashion industry. Pedro has been published in various magazines and newspapers, including *Toronto Life*, *Zoomer*, and the *Globe and Mail*. His blog, *The Hogtown Rake*, extensively covers style and traditional sartorial craftsmanship in Canada and around the world. Pedro has also produced and hosted podcasts about men's style and fashion history, has taught men's style seminars, and has worked as a menswear consultant. He lives in Toronto with his wife, their son, and a Wheaten terrier named Molly.